Thomas Garrett

William Still

Just Over *the* Line: Chester County *and the* Underground Railroad

A catalogue to accompany an exhibition organized by the Chester County Historical Society.

William C. Kashatus

Chester County Historical Society
West Chester, Pennsylvania

Published in cooperation with
Penn State University Press
University Park, Pennsylvania

This catalogue accompanies an exhibition held at Chester County Historical Society February 7, 2002 to December 31, 2002.

Book design by Suzanne DeMott Gaadt, Gaadt Perspectives, LLC
Printed and bound by Pearl Pressman Liberty Communications Group

ISBN: 0 - 929706 - 17 - X

Endpapers, Figure 1: CHARLES T. WEBBER'S *Underground Railroad,* 1893. (COURTESY OF CINCINNATI ART MUSEUM)

For *Jim McGowan,* whose scholarship on Thomas Garrett and the Eastern Line has contributed significantly to our understanding of the Underground Railroad.

Table *of* Contents

Foreword

The issue of race remains the great on-going tragedy of the American experience. Race was at the core of our costly Civil War. Slavery, Jim Crow, segregation, lynchings: all are stains on our nation. The Underground Railroad, civil disobedience, the Civil Rights movement, interracial cooperation, non-violence: all represent what Abraham Lincoln called "the better angels of our nature." American history, especially in the twentieth century, has been a progressive effort to let those better angels scrub the stains from our national conscience.

In the nineteenth century, the Underground Railroad was the first national and bi-racial effort to address the issue of race—an organized and deliberate violating of the law to help fellow Americans to escape slavery. Chester County was uniquely situated to play an important role in this movement, and it is this fascinating story that Chester County Historical Society seeks to tell through this publication and the exhibit it accompanies.

History museums like Chester County Historical Society are educational institutions that strive to make the past accessible, useful, and meaningful to the public. Exhibitions often celebrate and commemorate the past and in doing so create a collective memory that helps provide Americans with a common understanding of their past. Equally important is a museum's obligation to explore all aspects of the American experience.

History museums often must interpret difficult, unpleasant, or controversial episodes, not out of any desire to embarrass, be unpatriotic, or cause pain, but out of a responsibility to convey a full sense of our history. Certain words, objects, and ideas may be offensive—but we must let the past speak for itself, no matter how unpleasant that may be to read, see, or hear.

At Chester County Historical Society, we believe that the greatest contribution a history museum can make to public education is to provide visitors with tools to both celebrate and critically analyze our shared past. *Just Over the Line: Chester County and the Underground Railroad* is designed for that dual purpose.

This has been a collaborative effort involving scholars, community leaders, museum curators, and ordinary citizens from across Chester County and the nation, both black and white. We particularly want to acknowledge the help of our colleagues at the National Underground Railroad Freedom Center in Cincinnati, Ohio. The result of our efforts is a candid look at the critical role Chester County played in this important chapter in American history.

Since July 1999 William Kashatus and much of the CCHS staff has been engaged in *Just Over the Line.* Bill and our staff deserve our thanks and appreciation for bringing this vital episode in Chester County's history to life.

Roland H. Woodward, President and Director
Chester County Historical Society

November 2001

Introduction

Chester County, Pennsylvania was a region of tremendous paradox during the antebellum period. Located just north of the Mason-Dixon Line dividing the free and slave states, it was an important junction of the Underground Railroad's Eastern Line, being home to many Quaker abolitionists. The free black community and Friends formed a strong network of communication, transcending religious and racial barriers that allowed them to guide fugitives to freedom.

On the other hand, not all members of the Religious Society of Friends agreed to participate in the abolitionist movement, let alone the Underground Railroad. Some associated all antebellum reform with a liberal mindset that was destroying traditional Quakerism. Of special concern to these Friends was the worldly influence of non-Quakers who participated in secular reform activities. Others disliked dogma and made a strong commitment to such antebellum crusades as abolitionism, temperance, women's rights, prison reform, Indian rights and pacifism. Still others joined the anti-slavery movement but refused to violate federal laws against aiding runaways. These ideological differences eventually resulted in a schism among Chester County Quakers. Together with the pro-slavery element in the county, which was more than willing to kidnap runaways and sell them back into bondage for the bounty they would receive, the Quakers' divided sentiment presented many challenges for runaways.

Predictably, Chester County was not a safe Northern haven for fugitives, as the historiography suggests, but rather "a dangerous stop in a hotbed of abolitionism" where conductors took "grave risks as they delivered their passengers to the county's stations."[1]

The polarization of Chester County's white residents reflects the larger national division over slavery and challenges the historical myths associated with the Underground Railroad. Often, the story is told in the context of a free North and a slaveholding South. It assumes that all members of the Religious Society of Friends, also called "Quakers," were unified in their opposition to slavery and credits them, along with other white abolitionist operators, with the success of the clandestine enterprise. Fugitives, on the other hand, are generally depicted as helpless, frightened passengers, who took advantage of a well-organized network. Free black involvement is often chronicled through the best-known conductors like Harriet Tubman or orators like Frederick Douglass. We are left with a mix of historical fact, enhanced by over 150 years of mythology, giving us accounts of anti-slavery solidarity and focussing on daring rescues, ingenious hiding places, and great escapes.[2]

Because the Underground Railroad operated in secrecy and has few remaining records, many basic facts about its history are unknown. No one knows, for example, how many fugitives successfully fled from bondage along its invisible tracks. Nor is there any reliable source for the origins of the term "Underground Railroad," being based largely on anecdotal information handed down across the generations. According to one legend, two slave catchers tracking a fugitive through Kentucky lost all trace of the runaway when they crossed the Ohio River. In their bewilderment, they allegedly exclaimed, "There must be an underground railroad somewhere!"[3]

Properly defined, the "Underground Railroad" was a pseudonym for the clandestine movement of African-American slaves escaping out of the South to a loosely organized network of abolitionists who assisted them in their search for freedom in the North. While the enterprise began sometime during the eighteenth century after the abolition of slavery in the northern states, the Underground Railroad's greatest activities occurred between 1835 and 1865 and adopted the vocabulary of the railroad to disguise its illegal activity. Accordingly, the term "Underground" suggested a "secret," and "Railroad" a "method of transportation." Those who opened their homes to runaways were referred to as "station masters," and their homes, "stations." Others, who guided fugitives between stations were called "conductors." "Stockholders" played a less dangerous—and less conspicuous—role, but one that was extremely important. They provided the finances needed for bribes, transportation, food, and clothing. "Agent," was a more generic term, referring to *anyone* who worked on the Underground Railroad.[4] Most often, runaways escaped to the North using a loose network of routes through the southern border states. Those traveling in the East headed to such cities as Philadelphia, New York and Boston with the hope of becoming part of the free black community. Some fugitives continued on to Canada, where slavery was outlawed by Britain by the 1820s and where officials refused U.S. requests for their return.

Much confusion over the Underground Railroad stems from the lack of reliable sources as well as the unconventional use of those that do exist. Many accounts were written years after the fact by white abolitionists, who tended to emphasize their own heroics and omit the contributions of others, most notably the free black community and the fugitives themselves. Often these accounts were further embellished and replicated in subsequent novels, plays and, in some cases, historical monographs like R.C. Smedley's *History of the Underground Railroad in Chester and Neighboring Counties* (1883) and Wilbur H. Siebert's *The Underground Railroad from Slavery to Freedom* (1898). The result was an overemphasis on white abolitionist involvement, particularly among Quakers, and an over-simplification of a complex historical phenomenon that involved many religious groups as well as free blacks and fugitives themselves.[5]

William Still's *Underground Railroad* is a refreshing exception to less reliable accounts and continues to be widely considered by historians as the most accurate source on the topic. Still, an African-American man who was chairman of the Pennsylvania Abolition Society's Vigilance Committee, personally interviewed the fugitives who came under his protection. He recorded their personal histories: where they came from, who their masters were, how they escaped, why they escaped, and the dangers they encountered on their flight to freedom. Still carefully guarded the interviews until 1872 when he integrated his own observations as well as personal correspondence, excerpts from newspaper articles, minutes of anti-slavery meetings, and legal papers, and published them in an 800-page book.

Unlike many of his contemporaries, Still credits white abolitionists, free black people and fugitives with the success of the Underground Railroad. "As a general rule," he wrote, "the passengers of the Underground Railroad were physically and intellectually above the average order of slaves and were determined to have liberty even at the cost of life." Such fugitives as Henry "Box" Brown who freighted himself to freedom in a wooden crate and Ellen and William Craft who ingeniously disguised themselves as a slave master and servant and traveled by train and boat from the Deep South to Philadelphia, were not helpless individuals but very capable, self-reliant people who took matters into their own hands and, in so doing, impressed Still. At the same time, Still acknowledged the "Christ-like exhibition of love and humanity" extended by white abolitionists such as

Thomas Garrett, Lucretia Mott and William Lloyd Garrison, "who served the anti-slavery cause in its darkest days."[6]

More recently, Charles Blockson identified the aggressive and sustained activity of African Americans and their churches on the Underground Railroad.[7] Additionally James and Lois Horton have written important works on the northern free black community and its relationship with white abolitionists. Their research reveals a multifaceted and pluralistic free black society in southeastern Pennsylvania. While disagreement over leadership styles existed in that community, it did not preclude cooperation towards common goals within the free black community or with the white abolitionist community, particularly in such areas as abolitionism, involvement on the Underground Railroad, and securing educational opportunities for African Americans.[8]

Yet because of the popular focus on the white contribution to the Underground Railroad, historians have generally described a highly organized movement. In fact, organization was largely restricted to a few rural areas like Chester County and, in the 1840s, to northern cities like Boston, New York and Philadelphia where vigilance committees arose to combat the increasing threat posed by the federal government's enforcement of fugitive slave laws.[9] Especially after 1850, fugitives were not safe once they crossed over the Mason-Dixon Line because the new Fugitive Slave Law enlisted bystanders to assist the authorities and made the legal process simpler for slave catchers as they plied their trade. Under these circumstances, Chester County became a battleground in the struggle between disgruntled southern slave owners and northern abolitionists.

Just Over the Line: Chester County and the Underground Railroad, is an interactive exhibit at the Chester County Historical Society that will run from February through December 2002. It examines the Underground Railroad's Eastern Line, which ran through Chester County and into Philadelphia. It is a complex story that involves community conflict as well as moral decision making. It's broad conceptual framework integrates material culture, documentary history, oral tradition and folklore. While folklore and oral testimonies are sometimes controversial because they lack corroboration in written documentation, these sources are central to the African-American experience and must be addressed in any examination of the Underground Railroad. Because most slaves could not read or write, they were dependent on oral testimonies to tell their history. Additionally, storytelling was fundamentally important to most African cultures.[10] Accordingly, the research for the exhibit is based on primary source documentation, including Quaker Meeting minutes, journals, letters, and newspaper accounts. But it also draws on the stories, anecdotes, and folklore that have been passed down through Chester County's black families. While every effort has been made to distinguish the oral history from the documented material, both are critical to a multicultural understanding of the Underground Railroad.

Like the exhibit, this catalog is organized around the metaphor of a "line," which describes, at various times, the Mason-Dixon Line, or the behaviors of runaways, whites and free blacks with respect to the Underground Railroad. Accordingly, chapter one, "Drawing the Line," provides an historical survey of the Mason-Dixon Line and how that boundary came to represent the division between the free territory of the North and the slave territory of the South. Chapter two, "Crossing the Line," examines the flight of the runaways who crossed the Mason-Dixon into Chester County. Descriptions of those who fled, their motives for fleeing, and the culture of slavery they left behind are discussed as well as the routes they traveled. Pro-slavery activity is the subject of chapter three, "Holding the Line." Chester county was not only the scene of a fierce struggle between abolitionists and slave catchers who came North to reclaim their runaway slaves; it was a region where both white and black residents aided slave hunters in their search. Together these pro-slavery elements, supported by state and federal legislation, tried to preserve the status quo, reinforcing the legal right of the slaveholder to his property.

Chapter four, "Pushing the Line,"

explores the activities of those Chester Countians who heightened public awareness of the evils of slavery by joining abolitionist societies and taking part in the Free Produce movement. Most were Quakers, whose activities were inspired by a theological belief in the spiritual equality of all human beings and can be traced to 1688 when Friends issued the first petition against slavery in North America. Their decision to take part in these abolitionist activities, challenged the moral conventions of antebellum society that condoned slavery. At the same time, these abolitionists insisted on acting within the boundaries of the civil law, refusing to take part in the Underground Railroad itself. Members of Chester County's other religious groups also supported some level of abolitionist activity.

Those Chester Countians who participated in the Underground Railroad are discussed in chapter five, "Stepping Over the Line." These were radical abolitionists who defied the civil law, believing that the immediate abolition of slavery was in accordance with the divine will. While they sometimes acted as individuals, the radicals—black and white, Quaker and non-Quaker, male and female—often underscored their behavior with inflammatory rhetoric. Not only did they "step over the line" by breaking the law in their challenge of the peculiar institution, but also by creating a breach within their own churches over involvement in the Underground Railroad.

Even within this group there was division over the appropriate limits of resistence. Many Quakers, for example, gave food, clothing, shelter and transportation North to a fugitive, but refused to take part in armed struggle against the slave catchers. Many free black radicals, on the other hand, not only gave sanctuary to their enslaved brethren, but resorted to physical resistance when confronted by slave catchers and kidnappers. In these ways, the free black community "stepped over the line" by defending their God-given right to liberty, and often in a more aggressive fashion than their Quaker neighbors.

"Breaking the Line" of slavery is the topic of the final chapter. While black enthusiasm for the Civil War led many African Americans, both free and slave, to fight for the Union as well as for their own freedom, many of southeastern Pennsylvania's Quakers used more passive methods to affect Emancipation. Together they "broke the line of slavery" and created a new birth of freedom, not only in Chester County, but for the nation.

Just Over the Line concludes with an overview of race relations in Chester County during the 20th century and a brief statement on the implications of this history for the present. At a time when our country is looking to the past for examples of cooperation between white and black people to inform the current dialogue on race, the Underground Railroad is critical to understanding America's national character and the responsibility of the individual in the face of injustice. How, for example, did white people and free black people reconcile their involvement or non-involvement in a movement that was, according to civil law, "illegal"? What myths have developed about their involvement or non-involvement and why? In what ways did race affect enslaved black peoples' identity and their relationship to the free black community, the larger white community, and to the fundamental institutions of democracy?

Ultimately, *Just Over the Line* provides an historical framework for addressing these issues by exploring the complexities of black and white involvement on the Underground Railroad.

William C. Kashatus, Ph.D.
Chester County Historical Society

November 2001

Endnotes *to* Introduction

[1]Charles Blockson, *The Underground Railroad: Dramatic First-Hand Accounts of Daring Escapes to Freedom* (New York: Berkeley Books, 1987), 204.

[2]Larry Gara, *Liberty Line: The Legend of the Underground Railroad* (Lexington, KY: University of Kentucky, 1961).

[3]R.C. Smedley, *History of the Underground Railroad in Chester and the Neighboring Counties.* (Lancaster, PA: 1883), 34-35; and Wilbur H. Siebert, *The Underground Railroad from Slavery to Freedom* (1898) (New York: Arno Press, 1968 reprint), 45.

[4]James A. McGowan, *Station Master on the Underground Railroad: The Life and Letters of Thomas Garrett.* (Moylan, PA: Whimsie Press, 1977), 5.

[5]Larry Gara, "Some Lessons from the Underground Railroad," in *New Historical Perspectives: Essays on the Black Experience in Antebellum America,* edited by Gene Lewis. (Cincinnati: Cincinnati Historical Society, 1984), 39; and Carol Kammen, "The Underground Railroad and Local History," *History News* (Spring 1999); 3.

[6]William Still, *The Underground Railroad* (1872) (reprinted by Johnson Publishing Company of Chicago, 1970), xiii.

[7]See Charles L. Blockson, *The Underground Railroad in Pennsylvania* (Jacksonville, NC: Flame International, 1981); *Escape from Slavery: The Underground Railroad* (Washington D.C., 1984); and *Hippocrene Guide to the Underground Railroad* (New York: Hippocrene Books, 1994).

[8]James O. Horton and Lois E. Horton, *In Hope of Liberty: Culture, Community and Protest Among Northern Free Blacks, 1700-1860.* (New York: Oxford University Press, 1997); and *Black Bostonians: Family Life and Community Struggle in the Antebellum North.* (New York: Homes & Meier, 1999, revised edition).

[9]Gara, "Some Lessons," 42.

[10]Cuesta Benberry, "The Heritage of an Oral Tradition: The Transmission of Secrets in African American Culture," in Jacqueline L. Tobin and Raymond G. Dobard, *Hidden in Plain View: The Secret of Quilts and the Underground Railroad* (New York: Doubleday, 1999), 1 - 3; and John W. Blassingame, editor, *Slave Testimony: Two Centuries of Letters, Speeches, Interviews and Autobiographies* (Baton Rouge, LA: Louisiana State University, 1977).

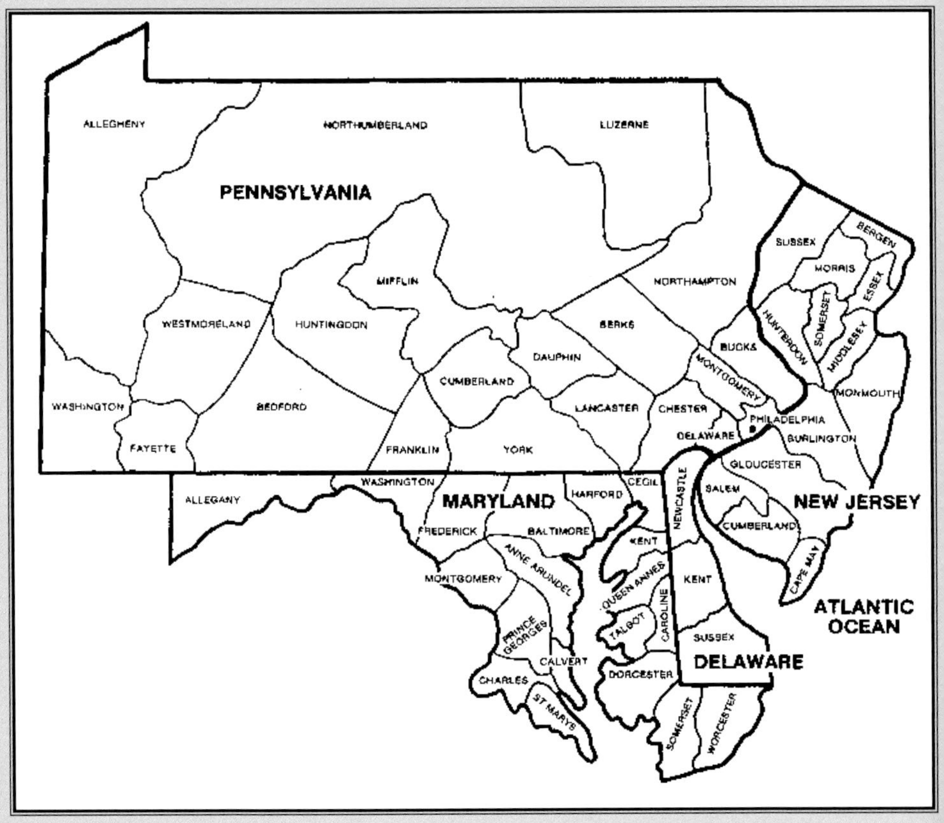
ALLEGHENY
NORTHUMBERLAND
LUZERNE
PENNSYLVANIA
MIFFLIN
NORTHAMPTON
WESTMORELAND
HUNTINGDON
BERKS
BUCKS
DAUPHIN
MONTGOMERY
CUMBERLAND
WASHINGTON
BEDFORD
LANCASTER
CHESTER
PHILADELPHIA
DELAWARE
FAYETTE
FRANKLIN
YORK
SUSSEX
BERGEN
MORRIS
ESSEX
HUNTERDON
SOMERSET
MIDDLESEX
MONMOUTH
BURLINGTON
GLOUCESTER
SALEM
CUMBERLAND
NEW JERSEY
CAPE MAY
ALLEGANY
WASHINGTON
MARYLAND
HARFORD
CECIL
FREDERICK
BALTIMORE
KENT
NEWCASTLE
ANNE ARUNDEL
MONTGOMERY
QUEEN ANNES
KENT
CAROLINE
TALBOT
PRINCE GEORGES
CALVERT
SUSSEX
ATLANTIC
OCEAN
DELAWARE
CHARLES
DORCESTER
ST MARYS
SOMERSET
WORCESTER

I.

Drawing *the* Line

On March 4, 1681, King Charles II of England granted William Penn a new world colony to pay off a debt the Crown had owed to Penn's father, an admiral in the King's navy.[1] But the boundaries of the 45,000 square mile tract were haphazardly laid, causing an overlapping land claim with Cecilius Calvert, the second Lord Baltimore, who had established the colony of Maryland a half century earlier in 1632. While Calvert set the northern boundary of his colony at the fortieth degree of latitude, Penn recognized the southern border of his territory as the same latitude. In theory, the arrangement seemed workable. In fact, it was mathematically and geographically impossible because there was an overlap of almost thirteen miles claimed by both proprietors.

Figure 2: 19th Century map of the Mason Dixon Line, which formed the boundary between Pennsylvania and Maryland, and the western and southern borders of Delaware; and Harlan House, located in Embreeville, was occupied by Mason and Dixon in 1764. (Photo by Edgar J. Parker, ca. 1905)

When navigational instruments revealed that Penn's provincial capitol at Philadelphia was actually located in Maryland, the Quaker proprietor attempted to establish rights to the disputed territory by encouraging settlement there and informing earlier settlers that they were residents of Pennsylvania and should start paying him taxes. Calvert retaliated by employing similar tactics.[2] The wrangling continued for three generations.

Not until 1763 did the Penn and Calvert families resolve the controversy by hiring Charles Mason and Jeremiah Dixon to locate and mark the boundary line. Both men were young, English astronomer-surveyors who brought an adventuresome spirit to the formidable task that awaited them. Their first step was to fix, by the stars, the southernmost point of Philadelphia. Theoretically, the boundary they were seeking lay 15 miles due south of the city, but such a line would have ended in New Jersey. Therefore, the two men sought another reference point west of the city so that the 15 mile limit would clear the "Great Arc" that formed the northern boundary of Delaware and come close enough to Pennsylvania.

On January 7, 1764, Mason and Dixon found the site they wanted in Chester County, on farmland owned by John Harlan. There they set up camp and spent several months "reading the stars." Both surveyors realized that determinations in longitude required accurate timings of celestial events at one place for comparison with the timings of celestial events at a reference point. They reasoned that they could find such a reference point by measuring changes in Polaris, the North Star. One degree of movement on the earth in a due south direction would cause Polaris to move one degree closer to the northern horizon.

In early March, Mason and Dixon discovered the reference point, having determined that they were, in fact, the same latitude as Philadelphia's southern boundary, and placed a rectangular slab of white quartz in the ground as a marker. This so-called "Star Gazer's Stone," would, in later years gain national significance as the point at which future surveys of federal land west of the Ohio-Pennsylvania line ultimately rested.

Having fixed the latitude of the boundary at 39 degrees and 44 minutes, the two

Figure 3, Catalog 22: Compass. Between 1764 and 1767, two English surveyors, Charles Mason and Jeremiah Dixon, used a compass like this one to plot the boundary between Pennsylvania and Maryland to resolve a long-standing conflict between the two colonies. The magnetic needle of the compass points in a northerly direction when aligned with the magnetic field of earth and allowed the two surveyors to fix the dividing line at 39 degrees and 44 minutes.

surveyors proceeded westward, placing stones every mile along the way. By 1767, they had reached beyond the present western terminus of Maryland, but were finally forced to turn back in the face of continued Indian threats. It wouldn't be until 1769 that the Mason-Dixon Line was run to the Ohio River by other surveyors.[3] In 1780, when the Pennsylvania Assembly passed a law calling for the gradual abolition of slavery, the Line assumed a more infamous status as the boundary between freedom and slavery.[4]

Slavery had never been a large scale institution in Chester County, or in Pennsylvania for that matter. Although William Penn's *Frame of Government* did not ban the institution or the slave trade, he, like many of the early Quakers settlers, was ambivalent about it, believing slavery to be economically beneficial but morally indefensible.[5] In fact, most of the Quaker, Dutch, and German settlers preferred to farm their own lands, with the help of indentured servants.[6] Thus, slavery in Chester County assumed quite a different nature than in the City of Philadelphia, or the South where there were more slaves, many on large plantations.

The county's slaves were engaged largely in farming and related activities. Tasks were divided by gender and workloads varied by the season. Most black males worked in the fields during harvesting and planting. During the winter months they cut firewood, mended fences, constructed or repaired buildings and accompanied their owners on trips to Philadelphia or New York. Female slaves worked primarily in the owner's house, cleaning, cooking, spinning and taking care of children, though they might help in the fields during harvest.[7] Philadelphia's slaves, on the other hand, worked in a wide variety of jobs in virtually every sector of the city's economy. Women were primarily engaged in domestic duties for their owners, though they were sometimes hired out to wash clothes, wait tables and help out in taverns and inns.[8] Males also labored in and around their master's homes as cooks, coachmen, and personal attendants, though a great many were sailors, stevedores, chimneysweeps and laborers. Those who were owned by artisans not only assisted in making furniture, barrels, houses and boots, but also learned the particular craft in which their owner was engaged.[9]

Whether in a rural or an urban setting, slaves not only served an important economic function, but also represented status symbols for their owners. Buying a slave cost much more than either purchasing a white servant's indenture or hiring a casual laborer. The wills and inventories of Chester County's wealthiest residents sometimes grouped their slaves with luxury items rather than with practical farming implements or livestock. Similarly, the most prominent Philadelphia merchants and artisans kept records of black footmen, coachmen, and personal servants in order to reinforce their elite status.[10]

In both rural Chester County and urban Philadelphia, black slaves worked side by side with their white masters, since most slaves were held singly or in groups of two or three. Only a few regularly worked with large numbers of their own race. They also lived under the same roof and associated with white laboring people on a daily basis. Thus, black people found it necessary to learn the rudiments of Anglo-American culture. It was difficult for them to maintain distinct African languages, religions or traditions over many generations, since they were geographically isolated from large numbers of their own people. After 1750, when masters increasingly began to purchase slaves directly from Africa, native African culture was reinvigorated in southeastern Pennsylvania through the influx of greater numbers of black people. During the next few decades, Philadelphia provided a setting within which black people could define their own African-American community.[11]

Figure 4: MARKER DEFINING THE BOUNDARY OF PENNSYLVANIA AND MARYLAND, ALONG THE MASON-DIXON LINE.

Chester County Historical Society

At the same time, however, slaves in southeastern Pennsylvania had less success in establishing and maintaining families than did slaves in the South during this period. In Philadelphia, African-Americans usually led fragmented lives, bearing few children, living together infrequently and forming short-term relationships, at best.[12] Since Philadelphia masters viewed slave children as an added expense, they actively discouraged their chattel from reproducing. "In this city, Negroes just born are considered an incumbrance only," wrote one Philadelphia slaveholder, "and if humanity did not forbid it, they would be instantly given away."[13]

Advertisements in the *Pennsylvania Gazette* offering slave children at a very early age confirm this observation, and many notices indicate that slave women were sold "for no fault but breeding."[14] In addition to these circumstances, the brisk slave market and high mortality in the city led to the breaking up of many slave families that did exist. Chester County slaves had more opportunity to have children, in spite of the physical distances between farms where family members lived. Familiarity with white society and close contact with their masters allowed them to manipulate their situations more easily in order to preserve family life. That does not mean that movement between farms went unregulated.

Slave codes also existed. The codes restricted the mobility of black people, preventing them from gathering in groups, and establishing curfews and patrols to enforce them. They also discouraged runaways by stipulating that slaves must carry a pass when away from home and, if caught more than 10 miles from their master without one, would, according to law, "be whipped by order of any justice of the peace on the bare back at the owner's charge, not exceeding ten lashes."[15]

On March 1, 1780, however, the Pennsylvania Assembly passed a law calling for the gradual abolition of slavery. The new law did not free those enslaved at the time, but it did stipulate that all "Negro and Mulatto children born within the state after the passage of the act" were to be freed when they reached the age of 28. Additionally, no new slaves could be acquired after 1780, and all slaveholders were required to register their slaves with the county courts.[16] Chester County, just over the Mason-Dixon Line, would now become a destination of choice for many fugitives escaping bondage on the clandestine route to freedom known as the "Underground Railroad."

Unlike most boundaries between states which had been determined by rivers and mountains, the Mason-Dixon Line was an arbitrary, man-made demarcation, running east-west along latitude 39°44'. But in 1780, the Line became something much more than a boundary between Pennsylvania and Maryland. It became the borderline between freedom and slavery. Now, crossing the Mason-Dixon north into Chester County, the fugitive saw possibilities before him: possibilities of hope, of human dignity, of personal freedom.

Figure 5, Catalog 10: Diagram of a Slave Ship. Slave ships were designed to use every inch of space to hold human cargo. Up to 20% of the cargo did not survive the long passage from Africa to the Americas also known as the "Middle Passage."

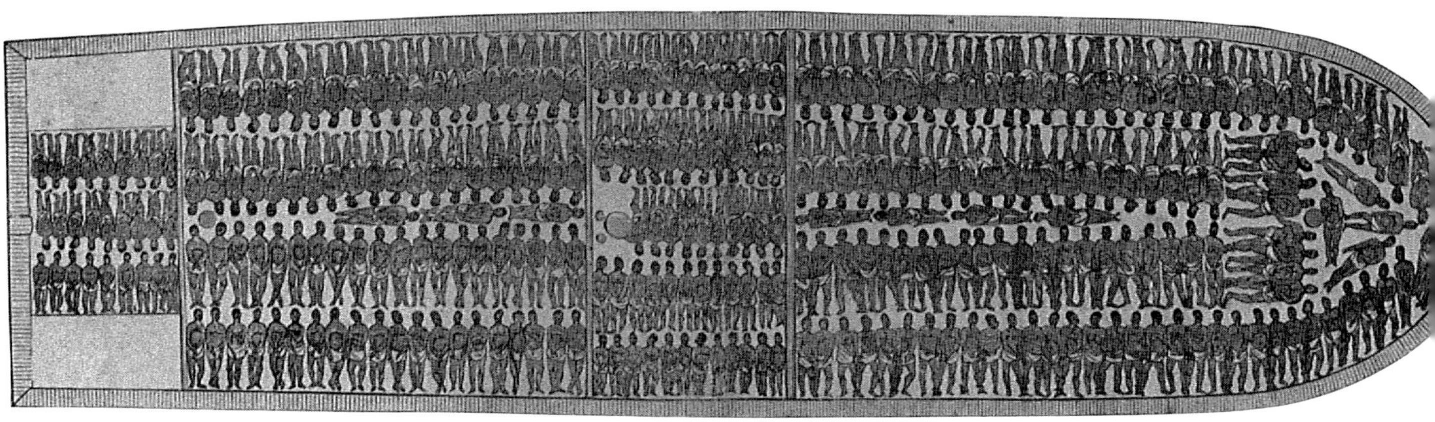

Endnotes *to* Chapter One

[1]Edwin Bronner, *William Penn's Holy Experiment: The Founding of Pennsylvania, 1681-1701* (Westport, CT: Greenwood Press, 1978), 21-22. In 1680 Penn petitioned Charles II for a new world province. Since the king owed his father's estate 16,000 pounds, Charles Stuart agreed to settle the debt with a grant of land. Additionally, Charles hoped that Penn might encourage the troublesome Quakers to leave England. Thus on March 4, 1681, Penn was granted a charter for the province of Pennsylvania.

[2]See William Penn, "Conflict with Lord Baltimore, June 1683 - August 1683, *William Penn and the Founding of Pennsylvania, 1680-1684: A Documentary History,* edited by Jean Soderlund. (Philadelphia: University of Pennsylvania, 1983), 277-307.

[3]William Ecenbarger, *Walkin' the Line: A Journey from past to present along the Mason-Dixon.* (New York: M. Evans, 2000), 15-19.

[4]"An Act for the Gradual Abolition of Slavery, 1780," transcribed by Isaac Gilpin in 1794. Copy in Chester County Archives.

[5]See William Penn, "The Frame of Government of the Province of Pennsylvania," (1682), *Founding of Pennsylvania: A Documentary History,* 120-33; Jean Soderlund, *Quakers and Slavery: A Divided Spirit* (Princeton: Princeton University, 1985), 34; and Sydney V. James, *A People Among Peoples: Quaker Benevolence in Eighteenth-Century America* (Cambridge: Harvard University Press, 1963), 114.

[6]Soderlund, *Quakers and Slavery,* 70.

[7]Joseph J. Kelley, Jr. *Pennsylvania: The Colonial Years,* 1681-1776 (New York: Doubleday, 1980), 39-45.

[8]Gary Nash, "Slaves & Slaveowners in Colonial Philadelphia," *William and Mary Quarterly* (April 1973): 248-252.

[9]*Ibid.*, 247-48; and Edgar J. McManus, *Black Bondage in the North* (New York: Syracuse University, 1973), 41-42.

[10]Ira Berlin, "Time, Space and the Evolution of Afro-American Society on British Mainland North America," *American Historical Review* 85 (1980): 47-54; and Darold D. Wax, "Negro Imports into Pennsylvania, 1720-1766," *Pennsylvania History* 32 (1965): 254-287.

[11]See Gary B. Nash, *Forging Freedom: The Formation of Philadelphia's Black Community, 1720-1840* (Cambridge, MA: Harvard University, 1988).

[12]Billy G. Smith and Richard Wojtowicz, *Blacks Who Stole Themselves. Advertisements for Runaways in the Pennsylvania Gazette, 1728-1790* (Philadelphia: University of Pennsylvania, 1989), 8; and Soderlund, *Quakers and Slavery,* 78-85.

[13]*Pennsylvania Gazette*: January 16, 1750.

[14]See *Pennsylvania Gazette* for advertisements on children which appear in the issues of: February 13, March 19 and December 6, 1750; November 29, 1770; and June 28, 1775. Notices for women appear in the issues of August 4 and October 24, 1765; and February 26 and May 21, 1767.

[15]Smith & Wojtowicz, *Blacks Who Stole Themselves,* 9; McManus, *Bondage in the North,* 73-88; and for quote see James T. Mitchell and Henry Flanders, editors, *The Statutes at Large of Pennsylvania, 1681-1801,* 18 vols. (Harrisburg: state Printing Office, 1896-1911) IV, 63.

[16]McManus, *Black Bondage in the North,* 73-88; and for quote see James T. Mitchell and Henry Flanders, editors, *The Statutes at Large of Pennsylvania,* 1681-1801, 18 vols. (Harrisburg: State Printing Office, 1896-1911), IV, 63.

Figure 6: **Runaway slave.** The figure of a runaway slave often appeared in the *Pennsylvania Gazette* and on the South's wanted posters.

2.

Crossing *the* Line

Rachel Harris was a slave of Mort Cunningham's, a Maryland planter. Cunningham was a severe task master, but one who was receptive to selling his slaves if the price was right. So it was that he sold Rachel to Henry Waters of Baltimore, a more benevolent but sickly master. Waters took her out of the fields and made her a house servant. He sent her to Sunday school to learn the rudiments of literacy and Christianity. He provided her with ample food, clothing and a more comfortable lifestyle. In fact, Waters gave "Cunningham's Rache" everything but what she desired most—her freedom.

One day, Waters asked her to accompany him on a voyage to New Orleans. During the trip he took sick and died. Rachel immediately seized the opportunity to escape. Being a tall, muscular woman with a nervous manner and a keen intelligence, she hid herself among a herd of cows as they were being taken ashore. Darting through the crowd, she disappeared, resurfacing a month later at the Chester County home of Emmor Kimber, a white Quaker station master on the Underground Railroad. There she remained for a considerable time as a paid cook, earning the esteem of her employers.

Figure 7: Judge Thomas Bell's house. Bell's house on the corner of Church and Miner Streets in West Chester, was the scene of Rachel Harris' daring escape. (Chester County Historical Society)

Chester County Historical Society

When Rachel married Isaac Harris, another former slave, she had finally found the kind of happiness that only freedom could offer. The couple settled in West Chester, occupying a small house on West Miner Street and there they lived happily for many years, until word of Rachel's escape got back to her former master Mort Cunningham.

Believing himself to be within his rights of recapturing his old slave now that Waters had died, Cunningham placed an advertisement in the northern newspapers seeking assistance for her recapture. When a man in West Chester learned of the reward being offered for "Cunningham's Rache," he informed the Maryland planter of her whereabouts. Cunningham notified a constable and proceeded to Rachel's house where she was arrested and taken before Judge Thomas Bell to prove that she was Cunningham's property.

While the proceedings were taking place at the judge's office at the southeast corner of Church and Miner Streets, Rachel asked to be excused for some fresh air. When permission was granted, the constable accompanied her outside into the backyard. Before he knew it, Rachel had scaled the seven-foot wooden fence that surrounded the yard with the agility of a cat.

Dashing out the alley and down Miner Street to High, she darted into a hatter's shop and out through the back building with the constable in heated pursuit. Springing over a dye kettle filled with boiling liquid, Rachel bounded over another wooden fence, catching a fleeting glimpse of Cunningham himself who had now joined the chase. Desperate for sanctuary, Rachel darted into the kitchen of John T. Worthington's house and pleaded with his wife to save her. She could trust these Quaker abolitionists, as she had for many years done their laundry and knew them to be station masters on the Underground Railroad.

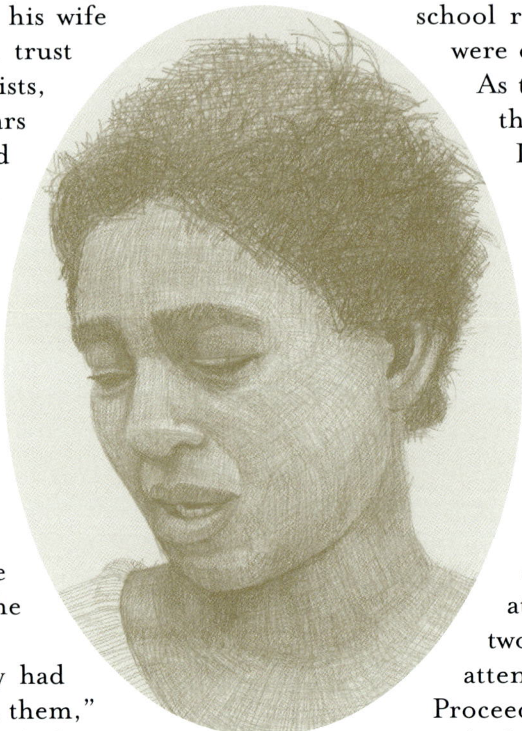

Figure 8: Artist's rendering of runaway slave Rachel Harris (sketch by Dane Tilghman).

Rushing up to Mrs. Worthington, Rachel cried: "For God's sake, take me in, save me, my master is after me!"

"Oh Rache! I can't imagine that he could have found you," she said, trying to calm the poor frightened soul.

"He is! He is! They had me, but I got away from them," Rachel insisted. "Oh hide me somewhere, quickly, please! I'd rather be cut to pieces than be returned to slavery!"

Convinced of her desperation, Mrs. Worthington immediately took her up to the attic where she hid her. Fastening the door to the hideaway, she returned to the kitchen to prepare dinner, pleased that she could give some measure of faithfulness to a former employee in all her distress.

Rachel, now secure among friends, peered through a small window and down at the streets below. She could see Cunningham and his vacant, dazed look as he sought to find her. Exasperated at her successful escape, both Cunningham and the constable returned to Judge Bell's office and told their tale. Afterwards they decided to resume their search the following day.

Learning of his wife's flight, Isaac Harris called on another white Quaker abolitionist, Philip Sharples for assistance. As Cunningham pursued any lead he could find the next day, Sharples devised a plan to secret Rachel out of town under the pretense of attending an evening lecture at the small Quaker school adjacent to the High Street Friends Meeting House.

About dusk, Benjamin Price, another Underground Railroad agent, drove his carriage into the Meeting House sheds as usual, hitched his horses and went into the school room where the students were engaged in their studies. As the hour approached for the lecture, he and his son, Isaiah, took their seats in the carriage as the others gathered for the talk. At the same time, Rachel was being dressed in male clothing by Mrs. Worthington. When the disguise was complete, she and John Worthington left the house and proceeded to the Meeting House, attracting no more attention than any other two men who would usually attend the evening lecture. Proceeding directly to the carriage sheds, Rachel joined Price and his son and set out on a forty-five mile journey to the Norristown home of William Johnson, another Quaker station master. The darkness of the night and a constant drizzling rain favored them with cover during the journey and they arrived safely the next day about ten o'clock in the morning.

Being a safe distance from West Chester, Isaac was reunited with Rachel that same day. After remaining with the Johnsons for some weeks, they moved on to Canada, a permanent sanctuary of freedom. Cunningham, on the other hand, only became more frustrated by his futile attempt to recapture his former slave. He continued his search in West Chester for two days, and then abandoned it.

Rachel Harris' aggressive role in her own

rescue raises some interesting exceptions to the typical profile of the fugitive slave, and suggests something about the pro-slavery attitude that existed in antebellum Chester County.

Most fugitive slaves were single, young men in their late teens and early twenties. Having no family responsibilities, they were not tied to the farm or plantation on which they worked and, in many cases, were openly defiant of their master's orders. Advertisements for such fugitives in *The Pennsylvania Gazette* abounded in the eighteenth century. They described the slave's name, age, personal circumstances, owner, point of origin, and physical appearance, including height, skin color, clothing, and noticeable scars or abrasions A typical notice appeared in the April 25, 1781 issue of *The Pennsylvania Gazette:*

Figure 9, Catalog 54: Graceanna Lewis of Kimberton operated an active station in northern Chester County.

Ran away from James Sharps in Sadsbury Township, Chester County, on the 10th day of April 1779, a remarkable likely Negro man, very black, named ABEL, about 24 or 25 years of age, 5 feet 10 or 11 inches high with a mole on one of his cheeks, his clothes unknown; it is supposed he harbours between New Castle and St. George's, or about Apoquinimink in Delaware State. Whoever takes up said Negro, and secures him in any gaol, or brings him to his master living at Hopewell Forge, in Lancaster County, shall have one ton of bar iron or the value thereof in currency, paid by Peter Grubb.[2]

After 1780, when Pennsylvania passed a Gradual Emancipation Act, most runaways came from Delaware, Virginia, and especially Maryland. Word quickly spread among slaves that the Keystone state was a safe sanctuary for runaways and many owners simply assumed that it was the destination point for those slaves who ran off. Isaac Taylor, a Kent County, Maryland planter, for example, took out a warrant for the arrest of his 28-year-old slave Perry at West Chester, "believing him to be in Chester County."[3] Similarly, Clarissa Purnell of Caroline County, Maryland, appeared before James M. Gibbons, Justice of the Peace at West Chester, on August 31, 1831, to appoint Charles Knight her agent in recapturing "a certain Negro man named Albert, about 26 years old, rather below the middle stature, of a yellow complexion, with a slight stoppage in his speech." Purnell claimed that Albert had been "held to labor and service" to her before his escape on July 31st. She was "informed that he is now living in Chester County." In compliance with the 1780 Law, Gibbons issued a warrant for the fugitive's arrest.[4]

Billy Smith and Richard Wojtowicz, in their work on eighteenth-century runaways, found that young, single men accounted for nine of every ten runaways who fled to or within the Mid-Atlantic region.[5] A more recent study by John Hope Franklin and Loren Schweninger reveals that male predominance among runaways continued well into the nineteenth century. During the period 1790 to 1816, for example, there were a total of 424 male fugitives whose escapes were noted in the major newspapers in Virginia, North Carolina, Tennessee, South Carolina, and Louisiana. Of those 424 male fugitives, 227 were in their twenties and 102 in their teens. On the other hand, only 81 notices for female fugitives appear during that same period. During the period 1838 to 1860, when the Underground Railroad witnessed its greatest activity, the number of advertisements doubled, but male predominance continued with 835 males and 212 females seeking freedom in the North. Of the 835 male runaways, 449 were in their twenties, and 166 in their teens.[6]

Women often were less willing to set out for freedom. Those with children generally remained in bondage to look after them, praying that they would not be separated by a sale. Those who did flee almost always traveled in the company of family or male fugitives. Often they risked being captured because authorities were on the lookout for groups of runaways. Nor could many female fugitives travel as quickly as males, especially with children in tow. Graceanna Lewis, a white Kimberton Quaker station master, offers a case in point. In October 1855, she gave sanctuary to ten fugitives, including a "mother, father and five children who escaped from New Chesterton, Maryland" in a horse-drawn carriage "stolen from their master." Recognizing the danger that suspicious neighbors posed, Lewis immediately divided the group and "sent the family by rail on toward Canada."[7]

According to John Hope Franklin, the "one to two thousand slaves that might have attempted escape each year represented a mere trickle from among the millions of slaves who were actually in bondage."[8] Nor did all of them travel along the Underground Railroad. In fact, most of the slaves who attempted to leave the plantation weren't running away at all. They were leaving for a brief period of time and intended to return voluntarily to the plantation. Generally, this kind of "absenteeisn" was done for a specific purpose, which could range from visiting a family member on another plantation, or to hunt, fish or pilfer food with other slaves, or simply to go into a nearby town to drink and play cards. Absenteeism was so common that most masters reponded to it with a mild punishment or ignored it altogether.[9] For the vast majority of slaves, the dream of freedom was never realized, and very few even attempted to achieve it.[10]

For those few who did achieve the dream, there were many reasons for running away. Among the most common was the death of a master, which caused great fear and apprehension among slaves about their own future, as well as the future of their family. Slaves were left at the mercy of heirs who might easily sell them for the profit they could make. Rachel Harris fits this description as she absconded immediately after her master's death. Having experienced the brutality of slavery under her previous owner, Mort Cunningham, she took the risk of achieving her own freedom. Similarly, a 38-year-old slave named Bob, belonging to John Evans of Uwchlan township, took the initiative to secure his own freedom. When Evans passed away in July 1784, Bob, who had been trained as a tanner fled with "a negroe woman" from his master's farm. Although Evans had promised to free him, Bob took no chances. Shortly after, Evans' sons offered a "three pound reward and reasonable charges" for the return of their father's slave.[11]

Another reason for running away was cruel punishment designed not only to instill humility and submission in the slave, but also to extract the most work from him. Slavery was, more than anything else, an economically profitable institution. Between 1820 and 1860, the peculiar institution nearly quadrupled from 1.5 million to 4 million slaves living in the border states and the Deep South. Although 75% of the white southern population had neither slaves or any immediate economic interest in the institution, the 10,000 families who owned 50 or more slaves made up a planter aristocracy who made their wealth by producing cotton.[12] They also fostered a severe type of worker discipline in order to maximize production and, hence, profit. Generally, field slaves awoke before dawn and worked an average day of 14 hours in the summer and 10 hours in the winter. Nor was it uncommon to work 18-hour days during harvest.[13] Masters, whether from the Upper South or the Deep South where cotton growing predominated, were not all alike. Some governed their slaves with great skill and were able to get the maximum work from them with a minimum of force. Others,

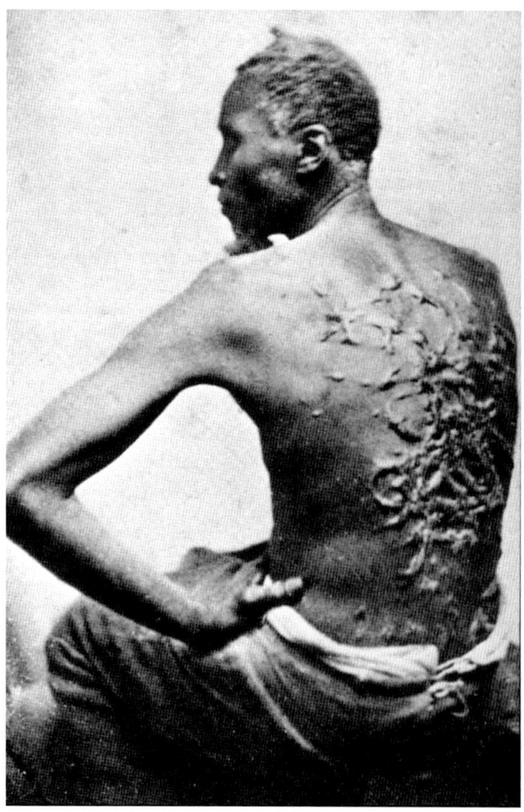

Figure 10, Catalog 20: Gordon, a runaway slave from Mississippi, under medical inspection before joining the Union army. His bare back reveals a network of scars, the result of several whippings during his bondage.

Figure 11: A slave mother being forcibly separated from her child. (Courtesy of Illinois Historical Society)

lacking the personal qualities needed to accomplish such submission, resorted to more severe punishments. Withdrawing visiting privileges to another plantation where a slave had loved ones, forbidding Saturday night dances, scheduling extra work, putting an offending slave in solitary confinement were all popular punishments. But none carried the weight of the whip. Planters instructed their overseers to give 20 lashes for ordinary offenses and 39 for more serious ones.[14]

Still other slaves ran away to avoid the sexual advances of their white masters. Few slave parents could protect their daughters from the sexual conquest of the owner. In fact, many slave men married women from another plantation because they did not want to be forced to watch as she was beaten, insulted, raped or starved without being able to protect her or his daughters.[15] Harriet Sheppard, the mother of three daughters and a slave in Chestertown, Maryland, "could not bear the thought of having her daughters bear the yoke of slavery" or her master's sexual advances. On November 1, 1855, she stole four horses and a carriage from her master and traveled North with five other fugitives, all male. Arriving in Wilmington, Delaware, they sought refuge at the home of Thomas Garrett, a white Quaker station master, who, in turn, channeled them across the Pennsylvania border into Chester County where other Friends cared for them on their way to Philadelphia.[16]

Of all the reasons for running away, however, the desire to be reunited with family was the most pervasive. Separation of slave families was common after 1820, as whites and their slaves migrated into the Tennessee and Mississippi River Valleys. Such forceable separation, according to John Hope Franklin, "probably destroyed one out of every three slave marriages and one out of every three slave children under age fifteen was probably separated from one or both parents."[17] Fear of being sold away from loved ones caused almost constant worry. Slaves pleaded with masters not to separate them. Often, their appeals were ignored. The trauma of being separated from family for the slave should not be underestimated.

While the family had no legal existence in slavery, it did offer one of the most important mechanisms for survival. In the family, slaves found companionship, social standing, dignity and worth. They learned how to avoid punishment, cooperate with other blacks and maintain their sense of self-esteem. Predictably, child-rearing was one of the most important functions of the slave family. Parents cushioned the shock of bondage for their children, taught them values different from those imposed upon them by the master, and if threatened with separation, would even run away to keep the family together.[18] Fearing the sale of her two children, Mary, a 33 year-old slave of John Ennis of Georgetown, Delaware, absconded with them in the winter of 1854. Convinced that her "daughters were to be sold further South," Mary and the girls made their way to West Chester, where they were passed on to the offices of the Pennsylvania Anti-Slavery Society in Philadelphia and eventually found freedom in Canada.[19]

Figure 12: HARRIET TUBMAN. (CA. 1820 - 1913) (COURTESY OF LIBRARY OF CONGRESS)

Regardless of their reason for escape, fugitives slaves traveling the Eastern Line of the Underground Railroad could find assistance among sympathetic abolitionists who would guide them from station to station. The best known of these so-called "conductors" was Harriet Tubman. Born into slavery on a Maryland plantation, Tubman escaped when she was in her twenties, vowing to help her family and other slaves secure freedom. She allegedly returned to the South on nineteen separate occasions to guide fugitives to the North. Having escorted more than an estimated 300 individuals out of bondage, Tubman was called the "Moses of Her People" and slaveholders supposedly set a reward of $40,000 for her capture.[20]

Thomas Garrett, the most active white Quaker abolitionist on the Eastern Line, worked closely with Tubman from 1845 to 1860 and estimates that she "passed through my hands 60 to 80 persons from Maryland."[21] Speaking with great admiration for her dangerous journeys to the North, Garrett once claimed that "Harriet has a good deal of the old-fashioned Quaker about her", being a "firm believer in a spiritual manifestation." She once confided to him that "God will preserve me from harm in all my journeys, 'cause I never go anywhere without His consent."[22] To be sure, Tubman believed that Garrett's assistance was the result of the Divine will as well.

Whenever she approached him for funding, she would greet the Wilmington Quaker with the phrase: "God has sent me to you for money and a new pair of shoes." On one occasion though, Garrett, playing devil's advocate, responded: "Harriet, art thou sure thou art not deceived? I cannot find money enough to supply all God's poor. I had five here last week and had to pay 8 dollars to clothe and forward them."

"God never fools me," she insisted. "Now I'm sure you've got enough money to pay for a pair of shoes and to pay for my own and a friend's passage to Philadelphia." Impressed by her determination, Garrett gave her twenty dollars.[23]

Often a runaway's journey began as a desperate action. Whether they fled alone or in groups, fugitives usually traveled under the cover of darkness. Most runaways also left in the warmer months of the year to avoid the obstacles of heavy snows, ice jams or thick fogs on the rivers and coasts. Spring, summer and fall not only afforded better traveling conditions, but also food as sustenance could be found in the small game, fruits, and vegetables that could easily be acquired in flight.[24]

According to folklorists, some slaves communicated their intentions of escape through songs whose words contained secret messages. In coded spirituals, slaves expressed their longing for freedom as well as plans and directions for the journey North. Tubman herself used the song "Steal Away to Jesus" to alert slaves that she was in the area and referred to "Jesus" as an open invitation for the slave to "steal away to freedom." Accordingly, those who decided to go with her would sing that same spiritual to alert family and friends of their impending departure. "Follow the Drinking Gourd" was a secret metaphor for the "Big Dipper," which served as a directional to the North. Runaways could follow this so-called "North Star" over mountains, through valleys and across unfamiliar territory, especially in a strange territory where fugitives didn't know who to trust. Other songs included "Wade in the Water, Children," which was a warning to avoid slave hunters by preventing their bloodhounds from picking up your scent, and "Let Us Break Bread Together," which told slaves to meet before sunrise on the east side of the slave quarters to plan an escape.[25]

Folklorists also claim that fugitives relied on feeling at night for moss which would grow only on the north side of a dead tree as another directional in addition to the North Star. When seeking refuge, they looked for a house with a wooden figure of a black slave holding a lantern near the entrance—a sign that the residence was a station on the Underground Railroad. If the lantern was lit, runaways were welcome to enter as no slave catchers were in the vicinity. An unlit lantern, on the other hand, signaled caution and fugitives would have to hide elsewhere until the danger had passed.[26] There is also a long-held theory that encoded quilts were used by slaves as both navigational tools and manuals to escape bondage.

Figure 13: Wilmington Quaker Thomas Garrett (1789 - 1871) collaborated with Harriet Tubman in assisting slaves to freedom through Chester County. (Chester County Historical Society)

Jacqueline L. Tobin and Raymond G. Dobard in their recent work, *Hidden in Plain View: A Secret Story of Quilts and the Underground Railroad,* report that oral traditions among African-American families maintain that slaves, free black people and white abolitionists used quilts made of familiar patterns to communicate the location of safe houses, dictate escape routes and convey other critical information by displaying them in plain view. "The beauty of the quilt code," according to Dobard, "was that it provided a cover for an enslaved people to recognize patterns that had meanings specific to them." Although the exact use of quilt codes is subject to conjecture, folklorists believe that the geometric patterns given in the code were intended as mnemonic devices, used to aid the slaves in memorizing directives before leaving the plantation. The names of the quilt pattern themselves functioned as metaphors in the code. For example, when the "Monkey Wrench" quilt was displayed, it was a signal to pack one's "tools" to prepare for the difficult journey to freedom, or a symbolic representation of the home belonging to someone who could be used as a "tool" in the escape process. Similarly, the "Bear's Paw" quilt was a code to follow the tracks of a bear through the mountains of western Pennsylvania to refuge in the eastern part of the state among Philadelphia's Quakers, who referred to that same quilt pattern as the "Hand of Friendship."[27]

Charles Blockson, however, cautions against the interpretation of quilt patterns as encoded messages for the Underground Railroad. While he admits that slaves "documented certain information about family history in their quilts, there is no documentation to prove that quilt codes were used as directionals on the Underground Railroad."[28]

Geographically, Chester County was an ideal sanctuary for fugitive slaves. Located just above the Mason-Dixon Line which divided free and slave states, the region was defined by a series of parallel hills, whose thickly-wooded slopes offered an natural avenue of escape as well as effective concealment for runaways.[29] Routes for the Underground Railroad came through both Delaware and Maryland. A "northern route" entered Lancaster County from Maryland by way of Fulton, then to the north through East Drumore, Eden, Paradise, and Salisbury, then into Chester County by way of Honeybrook and contin-

Figure 14: 19TH CENTURY MAP OF PENNSYLVANIA, NEW JERSEY & MARYLAND SHOWING LOCATION OF CHESTER COUNTY, JUST OVER THE MASON-DIXON LINE.

ued through to Phoenixville, then to Norristown and then to Philadelphia. Another major route cut through the center of Chester County, extending from Wilmington into Kennett, East Marlborough, Newlin, Downingtown, Lionville, Kimberton, and Phoenixville. Still another major route headed in an easterly direction, beginning at Wilmington and extending through Kennett, East Bradford, West Chester, Willistown, then to Philadelphia.[30] While these three lines formed the major routes of the Underground Railroad through Chester County, there were many other secondary paths a fugitive could travel.

Once he reached Kennett, just over the Mason-Dixon Line, the particular route a fugitive took depended largely on circumstance. Since Kennett was like the hub of a wagon with spokes leading in all directions, runaways had many choices open to them. Roads led east to Philadelphia and New Jersey; north to West Chester, Downingtown, Phoenixville, Lionville and Kimberton; northwest to Ercildoun and Coatesville; west to Avondale, West Grove, and on into Lancaster County. To the south were the villages of New Garden, Landenberg and Hockessin, Delaware. Similarly, once a fugitive reached Phoenixville, he could cross the Schuylkill River at Port Providence, or at Perkiomen Junction and head for one of many stations at Norristown. Consequently, if there was no space available at one station, the route could easily be altered to accommodate that problem. Alternative stations were often used when a fugitive was being pursued, as well, if only to avoid predictability. In most cases, the destination was Philadelphia, where a sizeable black population offered camouflage to a fugitive.

While many of Chester County's white residents were not abolitionists, the region was also home to a sizeable Quaker population, and thus had more stations than most of the other surrounding counties.

Sympathetic to the slave's plight, individual Friends, along with non-Quakers and free blacks, formed a loosely-organized network of stations, guiding runaways along the route to freedom. Among the documented stations, by township, were:[31]

Caln: Seymour Williamson, Grovner & Hannah Marsh, T.Vickers
Downingtown: Zebulon Thomas, Dr. J.K. Eshelman
East Fallowfield: James Fulton, Jr., Gideon Pierce.
East Pikeland: Emmor, Abigail & Gertrude Kimber
East Marlborough: Simon & Sarah Barnard
Kennett: Issac & Dinah Mendenhall, John & Hannah Cox, Allen & Maria Agnew
London Grove: Jacob Lindley, Amos & Mahlon Preston
Newlin: Richard Barnard, Isaac & Thomazine Meredith, Mordecai & Esther Hayes
Penn: Benjamin & Hannah Kent, Hambleton family
Pocopson: Eusebius, Sarah & William Barnard
Sadsbury: Joseph Fulton, Moses Whitson, James Williams, J. William Thorne
Schuylkill: Lewis Peart, Elijah Pennypacker
Uwchlan: John Vickers, Wallace, Micajah & William Speakman
West Caln: Thomas Bonsall, Abraham Bonsall
West Chester: Benjamin Price, Samuel & Joseph Painter, Abraham and Mary Ann Shadd, Thomas Brown, William Everhart
West Marlborough: James N. Taylor
West Sadsbury: Joseph Haines, Dr. Augustus W. Cain
West Vincent: John & Esther Lewis, Graceanna Lewis, William, Edwin, & Bartholomew Fussell
Willistown: David & Nathan Evans

By the late eighteenth century, news spread among slaves in nearby Delaware, Maryland and northen Virginia that they had a reasonably good chance to secure freedom if they could cross the Mason-Dixon into southeastern Pennsylvania.[32] But fugitives would have to be crafty about planning and carrying out their escape. Often, the role of white station masters has been overestimated, and the fugitives' role underestimated. This is particularly true prior to reaching Wilmington, Delaware, where the Underground Railroad was much better organized than in Maryland and Virginia; regions where the danger of recovery was great. Fugitives had to be clever and resourceful to initiate their escape, and then navigate their way through hostile territory, as pro-slavery sentiment was often as strong north of the Mason Dixon Line as it was in the South.

Endnotes to Chapter Two

[1]See Graceanna Lewis, "Cunningham's Rache" quoted in Still, *The Underground Railroad*, 781-83; and "The Escape of Rachel Harris, as told by her master in West Chester in 1839," *Daily Local News*: September 27, 1883.

[2]*Pennsylvania Gazette*: April 25, 1781.

[3]Warrant for the arrest of runaway slave "Perry" by Isaace Taylor, Kent County, MD: February 20, 1830. Chester County Archives.

[4]Warrant for the arrest of runaway slave "Albert" by Clarissa Purnell of Caroline Co. MD: August 31, 1831. Chester County Archives.

[5]Billy G. Smith and Richard Wojtowicz, *Blacks Who Stole Themselves. Advertisements for Runaways in the* Pennsylvania Gazette, *1728-1790* (Philadelphia: University of Pennsylvania, 1989) 13. Smith and Wojtowicz examine 300 advertisements for 364 runaways that appeared in the *Pennsylvania Gazette* between 1728 and 1790. These advertisements focus primarily on fugitive slaves and owners in the Mid-Atlantic region and lend themselves to a systematic analysis of the age, sex, height, clothing and skin color of runaways.

[6]John Hope Franklin & Loren Schweninger, *Runaway Slaves. Rebels on the Plantation* (New York: Oxford University Press, 1999), 328 -332, 396. In this groundbreaking work, Franklin and Schweniger examine advertisements for runaways in 20 newspapers from North Carolina, South Carolina, Virginia, Tennessee, and Louisiana. They provide a "Runaway Slave Database" that covers an early period, 1790-1816, and a later period, 1838-1860. The data base consists of approximately 8,400 runaways, nearly half of whom were advertised during the two time periods.

[7]Graceanna Lewis to Esteemed Friend, October 28, 1855. Chester County Historical Society.

[8]Franklin & Schweninger, *Runaway Slaves*, 367; See also the following historians whose research confirms Franklin's belief: Charles L. Blockson, *Hippocrene Guide to the Underground Railroad* (New York: Hippocrene Books,), 12-13; Gara, *Liberty Line*, 16-17; William Dusinberre, *Them Dark Days: Slavery in the American Rice Swamps* (New York: Oxford, 1996), 142.

[9]Franklin & Schweninger, *Runaway Slaves*, 98.

[10]*Ibid.*, 116.

[11]*Pennsylvania Gazette*: July 28, 1784.

[12]John Hope Franklin, *From Slavery to Freedom: A History of Negro Americans* (New York: Alfred A. Knopf, 1980, fifth edition), 132-134. Franklin estimates that in 1790, there were less than 700,000 slaves in the United States. By 1830, that number had grown to more than 2 million, and by 1860, to 3,953,760, with the majority living on the Deep South's cotton plantations, which were producing 5,387,000 bales of cotton annually. At the same time, only 384,884 white southerners held slaves in 1860, the bulk of whom were small farmers, owning five slaves or less. Fully 338,000 slaveholders (88%) held less than 20 slaves. Thus, Franklin argues that the large planters exercised an economic and political influence clearly out of proportion to their numbers.

[13]Kenneth M. Stampp, *The Peculiar Institution: Slavery in the Ante-Bellum South* (New York: Vinatge Books, 1956), 34 - 85.

[14]Eugene D. Genovese, *Roll, Jordan, Roll: The World The Slaves Made* (New York: Vintage Books, 1976), 64-70.

[15]John W. Blassingame, *The Slave Community. Plantation Life in the Antebellum South* (New York: Oxford University Press, 1978 paperback edition), 82-86.

[16]Still, *Underground Railroad*, 311-12.

[17]Franklin & Schweninger, *Runaway Slaves*, 51.

[18]Blassingame, *The Slave Community*, 77-79.

[19]Still, *Underground Railroad*, 210.

[20]Sarah Bradford, *Harriet Tubman: The Moses of Her People* (1886), reprinted by Applewood Books, Bedford, MA, 1993.

[21]Thomas Garrett to Sarah Bradford: 6 mo. 1866. Quaker Collection. Haverford College.

[22]Thomas Garrett to Eliza Wigham: 12 month - 27 - 1856. Quaker Collection. Haverford College.

[23]Ibid.; see also Garrett to Wigham: 10-24-1856. Quaker Collection. Haverford College; and James McGowan, "The Psychic Life of Harriet Tubman," *Visions Magazine* (March 1995): 1-3. According to McGowan, Tubman's divine inspiration was actually a psychic ability, probably caused by a head injury she sustained at the hands of her master in the fall of 1848. While recovering from the injury, she overheard her young master negotiating to sell her and prayed to God to kill him. Her master died shortly after. Stricken with remorse, she prayed for forgiveness. During this ordeal, Tubman claimed to hear the voice of God telling her to "rise up" and escape, and that she was "chosen to free her people from bondage." Throughout the rest of her life, she would periodically fall into a deep, trance-like state without warning. She said that during these trances, God spoke directly to her soul.

[24]Smith & Wojtowicz, *Blacks Who Stole Themselves*, 11.

[25]Charles L. Blockson, "Escape from Slavery: The Underground Railroad," *National Geographic* (July 1984): 39; See also Blockson, *African Americans in Pennsylvania. A History and Guide* (Baltimore: Black Classic Press, 1994), 12-13; and Kim and Reggie

Harris, *Music and the Underground Railroad* (Philadelphia: Ascension Productions, 1984).

[26]Blockson, "Escape from Slavery," 14; and Cuesta Benberry, "The Heritage of an Oral Tradition: The Transmission of Secrets on African American Culture," in Jacqueline L. Tobin and Raymond G. Dobard, *Hidden In Plain View: The Secret of Quits and the Underground Railroad* (New York: Doubleday, 1999): 1-3.

[27]Tobin & Dobard, *Hidden in Plain View,* 25-33, 69

[28]See Blockson quoted in Renee Lucas Wayne, "Threads of History?" *Philadelphia Daily News:* March 2, 1999.

[29]Bob Hill, "Forests & Freedom: Forgotten Links in Pennsylvania's Underground Railroad," *The Resource* (A Publication of the Pennsylvania Department of Conservation and Natural Resources) Vol. 3, No. 2 (February 1999) 1-2. Once a fugitive crossed the Blue Mountains in the south-eastern part of Pennsylvania, forests provided ample protection from slave catchers. Often, runaways were directed to the more durable Appalachian Ridge, whose hills, forests and valleys were covered with pine, hemlock, and oak, affording a host of hiding places.

[30]*Philadelphia Public Ledger:* August 27, 1911.

[31]See David Evans, *Journal,* Chester County Historical Society, for the most complete list of Underground Railroad stations in Chester County.

[32]*Pennsylvania Packet:* October 22, 1789.

3. Holding *the* Line

Figure 15: Tom and Simon Legree from Uncle Tom's Cabin (Courtesy of Illinois Historical Society)

On December 30, 1851, Rachel Parker, a 15-year-old free black house maid, was kidnapped from the West Nottingham farm of Joseph C. Miller. Miller set out after the kidnapper and, a few days later, was found dead, hanging from a tree outside of Baltimore. Two weeks earlier, Rachel's 10-year-old sister, Elizabeth, had also been abducted from Mathew Donnely's farm in neighboring East Nottingham Township. The kidnappings were almost predictable.

Located just above the Mason-Dixon Line, West Nottingham served as a buffer between the slave and free states and, hence, received many fugitives. A slave catcher, eager to return home with a bounty, knew he had a good chance of finding a runaway in the region, even if he had no clear claim to the slave.

Both of the Parker sisters were taken to Baltimore where they were deposited in a slave pen to await their sale. While Elizabeth was sold to a New Orleans plantation owner for $1,900, Rachel remained in jail awaiting trial. West Chester Quakers tracked her down and filed a petition for freedom on her behalf.

The kidnappings made news throughout Pennsylvania. The governor appointed the attorney general, along with Judge Thomas Bell of West Chester, as counsel. West Chester Quakers raised $300 in legal fees for Rachel's defense, and more than 70 persons, many of them Quakers from the Chester County Anti-Slavery Society, were on hand to testify for her, though only 49 were called to the witness stand.

The counsel for the kidnapper, Thomas McCreary, who was also suspected of murdering Miller, admitted defeat. Indicted by a grand jury in West Chester for the kidnappings, McCreary was sent to Annapolis for extradition, which was promptly denied by Maryland's governor. Shortly after Rachel was released, a party of West Chester Friends rescued her sister Elizabeth by paying her New Orleans' master $1,500 to free her.[1]

The Parker kidnappings, part of a rash of such incidents in antebellum Chester County, reflected the pro-slavery sentiment in the region. Not only did slaveholders and catchers from neighboring Maryland and Delaware infiltrate the county's borders, but many Chester Countians themselves were hostile to the plight of African Americans. Together, this pro-slavery element "held the line" against efforts to completely abolish the peculiar institution.

Even after the passage of the Gradual Abolition Act of 1780, there was still a substantial slaveholding population in the county. According to the slave register of 1780, there were 142 slaveholders and a total of 470 African-American slaves in Chester County. Of all the townships, Oxford had the most slaves with 28, followed by Charlestown (24), Tredyffrin (23), and Londonderry (20). The oldest slave was a 78-year-old woman named "Nanny," who was owned by John Evans of London Britain, and the youngest was a one-month-old boy named "Tom," living in Goshen township. Over 64% of the adult female slaves were listed with children and as many as 42% lived with a black male, indicating that rural slave women in Pennsylvania were much more likely to live with their families than Philadelphia's female slaves.[2]

Chester County's slaveholders were a diverse group which cut across several different occupations. [See Appendix A: Chester County Slaveholders, 1780] Among them were physicians, including: Dr. Joseph Moore of Goshen township, (who held 3 slaves for life); Dr. John Davis of Tredyffrin, (1); and Dr. Branson Vanler of East Nantmeal (1). Military officers composed another significant group, including: General Anthony Wayne of Easttown (1); Colonel Thomas DeWees of Tredyffrin (1); Captain Alexander McCaraher of Pikeland (2); and Captain William Alleson of East Caln (3). There were also several judges, including: James Moore of West Nantmeal (5); Evan Evans of London Britain (6); Joseph Park, of Sadsbury (4) and a minister, the Reverend William Foster of Sadsbury (3). Among the largest slaveholders in the county were: John Bell of West Fallowfield (who held 8 slaves for life); John Evans of London Britain (9); William Moore of Charlestown (10) ; and Job Ruston of Oxford (10). Many of the slaveholders were tavern keepers and mill owners, who depended on more skilled slaves to help run their businesses.[3]

Figure 16: **Rachel Parker**, a free black house servant from southwestern Chester County, was kidnapped by slave catcher Thomas McCreary in December 1851. It was one of the first kidnappings to test the new Fugitive Slave law, passed by Congress a year earlier. (Courtesy of Lancaster County Historical Society)

Those who owned slaves realized the worth of them and were eager to recapture runaways. Alban Harvey of Birmingham township, for example, owned an eleven-year-old male slave who ran away on March 3, 1812, Harvey tracked the boy to Easton Maryland a week later, and brought him back to Chester County.[4] Others were eager to capture a runaway for the reward money it would earn them. In June of 1782, William Starrett of East Nantmeal took out an advertisement in the *Pennsylvania Gazette* for the recapture of a fugitive. Starrett stated that "a Negro man called Caesar, about 22 years of age" called upon him for food and shelter. Dressed in a blue regimental coat with red facings and black worsted breeched, the black man claimed that he fought with the Continental Army. Because the man was "disposed to sickness," Starrett placed him under the care of a physician. Doubting the truth of his story, the East Nantmeal resident took out the advertisement appealing to "any master to come, prove property, pay charges and take him away." Otherwise, Starrett intended to sell him.[5]

Both state and federal legislation protected the right of the slaveholder to reclaim his slave. Because the 1780 Gradual Abolition Act did not apply to runaway slaves, fugitives were detained in the county jail, until their owner was notified by newspaper advertisement. Then a fugitive could be reclaimed for a small fee as well as proof of ownership. If no slaveholder appeared, a runaway was sold or set free at the discretion of the local court.[6] A fugitive slave law, passed by Congress in 1793, reinforced detainment, declaring that "any owner, his agent, or attorney so empowered, might reclaim a fugitive wherever found." The measure also fined anyone harboring a fugitive slave $500.[7]

Growing abolitionist activity among the county's Quakers, however, made such strictures difficult to enforce. Pennsylvania's abolitionists had organized, in 1775, the Society for the Relief of Free Negroes Held in Bondage, a precursor of the Pennsylvania

Figure 17: Slave auction. Before the passage of the Gradual Abolition Act in 1780, slave auctions were not uncommon in the City of Philadelphia where some Chester Countians purchased slaves. (Courtesy of Illinois Historical Society)

Abolitionist Society, formally organized in 1787.[8] Both of these societies assisted slaves hoping to secure their freedom or that of their children. Once determining the merits of a particular case, the members, many of whom were lawyers, would press forward in the courts with those regarded as viable.[9] While their members did not attempt to achieve emancipation through judicial decree, they were always exploring ways to broaden the scope of the 1780 law, and proved rather successful.[10]

As early as 1786, George Washington, a Virginia slaveholder himself, commented on the difficulty of retrieving fugitives once they entered southeastern Pennsylvania. Writing of another slaveholder who traveled to Philadelphia to "attend a vexatious lawsuit respecting a slave of his," Washington assailed the Quakers for "attempting to liberate the slave." While he labeled their legal maneuverings as "repugnant to justice," the future president also gave a hint of his own ambivalence about slavery. "I hope it will not be conceived from these observations," he wrote, "that it is my wish to hold the unhappy people in slavery. I can only say that there is not a man living who wishes more sincerely than I do, to see a plan adopted for the abolition of it; but there is only one proper and effectual mode by which it can be accomplished, and that is by legislative authority."[11]

In fact, Washington's desire for a legislative solution had already begun to bear fruit in Chester County, where the number of slaves were declining as a result of manumission by the 1780 law. By 1800, there were only 58 slaves living in the county, a very significant reduction from the 450 residing in the region two decades earlier. Twenty-seven of the 58 slaves, or 46% were age 40 or older and would have been considered near the end of their productive life. These statistics indicate that Chester County slaveholders were not acquiring new, young slaves after 1780.[12] Certainly from an economic standpoint, slave labor was less profitable as well as less convenient than wage labor in an area such as southeastern Pennsylvania where the economy was more diverse than the cash crop farming of the southern plantation.[13] Many former slaves remained in Chester County becoming hired laborers or farmers, and seeking protection from the growing number of black churches in such areas as West Chester and Oxford. Others removed to Philadelphia, which, by the 1790s, had a free black population of nearly 5,000 and could boast of the largest urban concentration of free blacks in America.[14] Still others relocated further north, hoping to place a safer distance between themselves and the slave catchers who routinely patrolled Chester County in search of fugitives.

Between 1820 and 1860, the number of free blacks in Pennsylvania jumped from 32,153 to 56,949. This significant growth was due to natural increase, successful escapes, mulattoes "passing as whites," slaves purchasing their freedom, and the continuation of manumissions. Throughout the nation, however, the number of slaves also increased.[15]

The inconsistency mirrored a larger national conflict between the northern system of free land and free labor and the southern system of plantation slavery, especially after the Mexican-American War when the relationship of slavery to the acquisition of new lands became a hotly debated political issue in Congress. The conflict spelled nothing less than the future of the nation. Would the United States become a modern country, with an industrial economy based on free labor, or would it remain backward-looking, dependent on an agrarian economy based on slave labor?

In the past, the North and the South managed to settle their differences over slavery by political compromise. The questions of the slave trade and the number of slaves counted for congressional representation were resolved through compromise at the Constitutional Convention in 1787. Similarly, the Missouri Compromise in 1820 established a workable plan to balance the admission of free and slave states to the Union and also defined a geographic boundary (36° 30') in the Louisiana Territory to determine future decisions. Pennsylvania's politicians tended to accommodate southern interests as well, fearing that slavery would divide both the Democrat and Whig parties into northern and southern factions.

Whenever possible, political leadership in Washington and in Harrisburg ignored the growing sectional dispute. In 1826, for example, Maryland requested that the Pennsylvania state legislature pass a bill that would assist slave owners in retrieving their runaways. A bill of this nature was debated and passed both houses and the governor immediately signed it into law. The measure strengthened the 1793 fugitive slave law, which had been haphazardly enforced, by permitting the claimant to place an alleged runaway in the Pennsylvania jails pending his trial. At the same time, however, the new measure placed the burden of proof on the owner by requiring him to secure a warrant for the arrest, and produce evidence together with an affidavit subscribed before a justice of the locality from which the fugitive had escaped. While the legislature passed the act partly to appease Maryland's slaveholders, its primary objective was to "prevent the kidnapping of free people of color," which it did by imposing heavy penalties on those slave catchers who attempted to do so.[16]

Almost immediately, the Pennsylvania Anti-Slavery Society used every legal technicality possible to circumvent the law and secure emancipation for runaways. Realizing that the strength of popular sentiment could be turned to their advantage, a delegation led by anti-slavery Quakers besieged the legislature with petitions asking that fugitives be permitted trial by jury. Since the sympathies of the state's courts were usually with the fugitive, these abolitionists believed they could prevent a return to slavery no matter how clear an owner's title.[17] But their proposition was voted down by a decisive majority who believed that to allow a jury trial for a black person would nullify the United States Constitution.[18]

The abolitionists rallied by pressing the Pennsylvania legislature to pass a personal liberty law which would nullify the 1793 Fugitive Slave Law. They were unsuccessful until 1842 when the Supreme Court, in *Prigg v. Pennsylvania,* ruled that while a master could not be restrained by state laws from seizing his slave so long as he didn't disturb the peace, the state was not required to assist in the recapture.[19] Acting on this precedent, the state legislature, in 1847, passed a new measure limiting the slaveholder's rights. According to the so-called "personal liberty law," no judge or state official could take any case arising under the federal law of 1793, or issue a warrant for removal. If an owner or his agent attempted to wrongfully seize a black person—free or slave—on Pennsylvania

Figure 18: ZEBULON THOMAS HOUSE. ON APRIL 19, 1848, THE DAUGHTER OF A FEMALE FUGITIVE WAS KIDNAPPED FROM THE ZEBULON THOMAS HOUSE AT 330 EAST LANCASTER AVENUE IN DOWNINGTOWN. TODAY THE BUILDING IS A PUBLIC LIBRARY. (CHESTER COUNTY HISTORICAL SOCIETY)

soil, he would be charged with a misdemeanor and be subject to fine and imprisonment in the county jail. In other words, even if a slaveholder was clearly within his rights, he could expect no assistance from the state. If caught kidnapping, he would serve time in jail.[20]

Frustrated by abolitionist efforts, unscrupulous slave catchers continued to kidnap fugitives and sell them back into bondage. By the late 1840s, the kidnapping of runaways was common in Chester County. One of the most daring outrages occurred early on the morning of April 19, 1848. Three persons entered the home of Zebulon Thomas at 330 East Lancaster Avenue in Downingtown and proceeded to the third story, where a female fugitive and her little girl were soundly asleep. A scuffle ensued. The woman broke loose and made her way down the stairs to awaken Thomas, who arose and tried to restrain the men as they hauled off the young daughter. Being overpowered by the ruffians, Thomas watched helplessly as they carried off the child. Though he dressed and went in pursuit, his attempt to rescue the woman was also unsuccessful.[21] Although the young girl was traced to Maryland and recovered through purchase by West Chester abolitionist Dr. Sharples, the incident registered the sobering reality that slaveholders and their agents were determined to defeat the Underground Railroad.[22]

Even black people who had been born into freedom might be kidnapped and sold South. Contemporary newspapers recount the story of kidnappers breaking into the homes of free black people in Downingtown, West Chester, and Unionville. In March 1849, for example, Amos B. McFarlan and Solomon States of Downingtown decoyed a local free black adolescent by promising him a good job as a coachman. Instead, they kidnapped him and placed him in a Baltimore, Maryland slave jail to be sold into slavery. When the boy contacted his employer, who vouched for his free status, McFarlan and States were sentenced to solitary labor at the Pennsylvania State Penitentiary in Philadelphia. McFarlan was given six years and States, five on the grounds that he had been "used" by McFarlan. In addition, both men, who were also suspected of the earlier kidnapping at the Thomas home, were fined $500 and the cost of prosecution.[23] Not all of the kidnappings had such a happy ending, though.

In September 1849, for example, Tom Mickel, a free black laborer of West Marlborough was "taken off at midnight from his house" by a "company of Maryland pirates." The kidnappers took Mickel to Baltimore where they placed him in a slave pen to await sale. Two local white abolitionists, George Martin and Samuel Pennock, followed the kidnappers in the hope of purchasing Mickel's freedom. Instead Martin was jailed and Pennock "had to pay a good sum to get him out." Mickel was never recovered, most likely being sold into bondage.[24] The most heinous crime, however, occurred that same year at the Unionville home of Thomas Mitchell, a free black man who had lived in the county for more than a decade.

On August 21st, shortly after midnight, Mitchell's neighbors were awakened from their sleep by cries of "murder" and shrieks of distress. When they came to his aid, they found the door to Mitchell's house battered in, his wife "half-insensitive with fright lying within," and he was nowhere to be found. Near his fallen wife lay a pistol loaded with three bullets and the percussion cap exploded. Further investigation revealed that four men had seized Mitchell from his bed, handcuffed, and hustled him into a carriage while his wife sat and watched helplessly.

Before dawn, two parties were formed, one to search for the kidnappers at Wilmington, and the other to travel to Baltimore by railroad. Before either party could intercept the kidnappers though, Mitchell was taken to a Baltimore slave prison where he was sold to a trader and immediately sent South.[25] Even if Mitchell had been able to defend himself, there was no certainty that he would realize justice.

Free black people were vulnerable to the whim of the local courts. John Reed offers a prime example. Reed, who settled in Chester County in 1818, believed his new home to be safe from the arbitrary acts of kidnappers. But in 1821 two prowlers, who he believed to be kidnappers, awakened him in the middle of the night. Reed killed them. He was tried and found not guilty by reason of self-defense in one death, but was found guilty of manslaughter in the other and sentenced to nine years in prison.[26] The case is an example of the tenuous position blacks held in the Pennsylvania court system. While Reed was not executed or returned to slavery, he was, at the same time, not allowed to go free.

Southeastern Pennsylvania had become a legislative battleground over slavery. Southerners, in general, and Marylanders, in particular, resented Pennsylvania's circumvention of the fugitive slave law as well as what they believed to be the lax federal enforcement of it. They called for a stronger act and particularly wanted to end the protection that northerners gave runaways as they fled along the Underground Railroad to Canada. The Compromise of 1850 gave them what they wanted. Among the several measures of the omnibus bill was a stronger, more controversial fugitive slave act. Three provisions of the act, in particular, angered both black and white abolitionists. One did not require a jury trial for the alleged fugitive, and established special commissioners to decide special cases, making those cases administrative rather than judicial matters. Another provision made it mandatory for all citizens to assist in the enforcement of the act, or be "subject to a fine not exceeding one-thousand dollars, and imprisonment not exceeding six months."[27]

Many northerners considered the Fugitive Slave Law of 1850 a serious violation of personal liberties and constitutional guarantees, bringing the evils of the peculiar institution onto their own soil. Slaveholders hired agents to seize their runaways in the North. Young black people were particularly vulnerable to kidnapping, not only because they commanded a good price, but they were a better risk than adults. Rapid growth, combined with the hardships of slave labor, often made identification virtually impossible within a few years time.[28]

Just months after the passage of the infamous law, stationmaster Thomas Garrett wrote to William Lloyd Garrison, editor of the abolitionist newspaper *The Liberator,* about the "several free persons arrested as runaways" in Chester County. "Any white man here may arrest a colored man on suspicion of his being a slave and put him in jail," he stated. "If he is proved a slave, the man taking him up gets a reward. If free, the county pays the expenses and the poor black has no remedy or compensation for lost time."[29] Even worse, the new law seemed to encourage kidnappers, as the seizure of free blacks and fugitives alike seemed to increase because of the bounty money that was being offered.[30]

In southern and western Chester County information on fugitives employed as free black people would be passed on to such kidnappers as the notorious "Gap Gang," a band of "land pirates" who operated in the western part of the county and southeastern Lancaster County. Often, the kidnappers would invade a free black sanctuary in the middle of the night for their bounty.[31] According to the abolitionist C.M. Burleigh, who witnessed some of these raids, the members of these free black communities were, by 1851, "desperately resolved on self-defense against the land pirates, which have been let loose on upon them by the recent slave-catching law."[32]

Kidnapping plots were not limited to white southerners either. In fact, local lore accuses George Walls, a free black landholder and former Underground Railroad agent from Oxford, of collaborating with slave catchers by "decoying fugitives fresh from bondage to his house on various pretexts." By feigning friendship, Walls learned the "name of their master, his residence, and other necessary particulars." He would then communicate with the master, "telling him what time the fugitive would be at his house." When the slaveholder arrived, the "poor refugee would fall into the merciless clutches of his master."[33] Nor was Walls unique in this respect. Though not very common, spies and informers could be found among the free blacks who settled in small communities along the border of southern Chester County, just over the Mason-Dixon Line. Some of these "artful black villains roamed about, representing themselves as former slaves."[34]

Chester County's pro-slavery press seemed to condone the kidnappings by depicting free black people as a burden to northern society, constantly falling into trouble with the law. Throughout the 1850s, West Chester's *Jeffersonian,* known for its conservative Democrat political ideology, ran reports that highlighted black crime, such as the following notice: "Sam Smith, a young darkey, was arrested on Monday last in West Chester and taken before Squire Whitehead, who fined him $5 for disturbing a religious meeting."[35]

By 1860, *The Jeffersonian* had become openly hostile towards West Chester's free black residents. Citing the fact that the borough had only 500 blacks in a total population of some 5,000 people, the newspaper denounced the construction of a "large school edifice" for black children. "Why should our citizens erect such a school at a cost of $7,000, for the special benefit of these Negroes, while the younger children of the 4,500 white people are pent up in small, unhealthy rooms, the backs of churches and engine houses?" asked the *Jeffersonian.* "We suggest that a population that would sustain the building of a palace for a few Negroes, to the manifest injury of a larger portion of white children, is just the material to amalgamate with the slaves of the South."[36]

Another conservative newspaper, the *American Republic,* voiced its fear over the assimilation of southern slaves into Chester County's economy if emancipation ever occurred. "What would happen to your markets, your manufactures, your commerce, your rents and investment?" asked the editors of its readers. "Have you not measured the extent of the evil to yourselves and to your children?"[37] The *Jeffersonian* was even more sensationalist in its speculation of an integrated society. "Four million Negroes who are now slaves in the South will overrun Pennsylvania, not leaving an acre of our soil untrodden by their gizzard feet," predicted the newspaper's editors. "These dependent Negroes will come among us and what food or clothing they can not get by begging they will take by stealth." Raising the specter of white displacement in the labor force, the conservative newspaper called on "white mechanics and workingmen to protect themselves from the degrading and injurious competition of free Negro labor by opposing the election of Abraham Lincoln to the presidency."[38]

In effect, the Fugitive Slave Law of 1850 forced northern communities to confront the realities of the peculiar institution and the power of southern slaveholders. Chester County, just over the Mason-Dixon Line in free territory, would become a battleground for slave hunters and abolitionists alike. As the decade unfolded, the local struggle was intensified by national events such as the expansion of slavery into Kansas in 1854, the Dred Scott decision of 1857 which held that African Americans were "so far inferior that they had no rights which the white man was bound to respect," and John Brown's attempt to instigate a slave insurrection with his raid at Harpers Ferry in 1859.[39] These events raised a storm that made it certain that there could be no further accommodation between Northern and Southern interests.

Endnotes *to* Chapter Three

[1]*West Chester Village Record:* January 18, 1853.

[2]"An Act for the Gradual Abolition of Slavery, 1780." Transcription in Chester County Archives. See Soderlund, *Quakers and Slavery,* 84 for comparative circumstances of female slaves in rural and urban areas.

[3]*Ibid.;* For names of tavern keepers and millers who owned slaves, see John Bradley, *Around the Oak: Oxford, Pennsylvania* (Oxford, PA: Friends of Oxford Public Library, 1999), 5, 10 & 65; and Margaret L. Wold, *A History of West Whiteland* (Exton, PA: West Whiteland Historical Commission, 1982), 16-17.

[4]Alban Harvey, Diary: March 3 - 15, 1812. Chester County Historical Society.

[5]*Pennsylvania Gazette:* June 5, 1782.

[6]See Mitchell & Flanders, *Statutes at Large of Pennsylvania,* X, 71; and *Pennsylvania Gazette:* February 18, 1801.

[7]"An Act respecting fugitives from justice and persons escaping from the service of their masters," (1793) quoted in Edward R. Turner, *The Negro in Pennsylvania: Slavery, Servitude and Freedom, 1639-1861* (New York: Negro Universities Press, 1910), 231.

[8]See John K. Alexander, *Render Them Submissive: Responses to Poverty in Philadelphia, 1760-1800* (Amherst, 1980), 234-35; and Charles L. Blockson, *Pennsylvania's Black History* (Philadelphia, 1973), 1-8.

[9]Gary B. Nash & Jean R. Soderlund, *Freedom By Degrees. Emancipation in Pennsylvania and its Aftermath* (New York: Oxford University, 1991), 119.

[10]Ibid.

[11]George Washington to Robert Morris, April 12, 1786. *George Washington Papers,* Library of Congress.

[12]Statistics taken from the *Pennsylvania Septennial Census Returns, 1779-1863:* Chester County, 1800. Microfilm in the Pennsylvania State Archives, Harrisburg, PA. The Septennial Census is an enumeration of taxable inhabitants which was taken every seven years. The Census lists slaves in each county, by township. While the amount of information varies greatly from county to county, Chester County was consistent in listing the number of slaves in each township as well as their age and gender. It is important to note that few slaves under age 20 are listed in the census, indicating that only the slaves born before November 1780 were enumerated since they were considered "slaves for life." Children of slaves born after that date were to be freed upon their 28th birthday in accordance with the Gradual Emanicipation Act of 1780. Although these children were held in bondage for 28 years, they were designated as "servants" and, as such, were not counted in tax and census listings as "slaves."

[13]Nash & Soderlund, *Freedom By Degrees,* 142-43.

[14]*Dunlap's Daily Advertiser:* April 5, 1793.

[15]Turner, *Negro in Pennsylvania,* 253.

[16]*Ibid.* 233-34.

[17]*Ibid.,* 235.

[18]*Ibid.,* 236. The Pennsylvania legislators who voted down the measure found support with an 1819 ruling of the Pennsylvania Supreme Court which argued that a jury trial was not required for blacks because the intent of the Constitution was to protect the property rights in slaves and anyone with a right to freedom could get a jury trial in their own state. Not until 1836, however, did the New Jersey Supreme Court support the right of a jury trial for a slave. A year later, it passed a law requiring such a jury trial if a fugitive demanded it.

[19]Blockson, *Underground Railroad in Pennsylvania,* 189.

[20]Turner, *Negro in Pennsylvania,* 237-39.

[21]*American Republican:* April 25, 1848; and Mary B. Thomas to "Dear Friend," April 19, 1848, quoted in Still, *Underground Railroad,* 609-610.

[22]*Jeffersonian:* May 16, 1848.

[23]"Trail of Amos B. McFarlan and Solomon States of Downingtown," *Pennsylvania Freemen:* August 16, 1849.

[24]Magdeline Pyle to George Pyle, September 23, 1849, Chester County Historical Society.

[25]*Pennsylvania Freeman:* September 6, 1849.

[26]Chester County Court of Quarter Sessions, Indictments January 1821. Commonwealth vs. John Reed. Chester County Archives, West Chester, Pa.

[27]"Fugitive Slave Act, 1850" reprinted in Still, *Underground Railroad,* 355-60.

[28]*Minutes of the Proceedings of the Fourteenth American Convention for Promoting the Abolition of Slavery* (Philadelphia, 1816, 7-8.

[29]Thomas Garrett to William Lloyd Garrison, December 5, 1850, Boston Public Library.

[30]There were at least a dozen kidnappings of free blacks from Chester County reported in the local newspapers in the six months since the passage of the Fugitive Slave Law of 1850. See *Pennsylvania Freeman:* February 20, 21, 25; April 3, 6, 17, 1851; *Village Record:* March 10, 21; April 18, 25, 1851; and *American Republican:* March 25, 28, 1851.

[31]*Village Record:* March 27, 1860; See also Albert J. Wahl, "The Congregational or Progressive Friends in the Pre-Civil War Reform Movement," (Ph.D. Dissertation, Temple University, 1951), 296; and

W.U. Hensel, "The Christiana Riot and the Treason Trials of 1851," *Lancaster Historical Society Papers,* XV (October 1911): 15.

[32]*Pennsylvania Freeman:* February 20, 1851.

[33]See William Parker, "Freedman's Story," *Atlantic Monthly* 17 (February 1866), 166; and Walter and Mary Dyson, "George Wall" (unpublished manuscript, 1959), 19. Special Collections, Lincoln University Library. Wall descendants Hersey Gray, Brenda Boddy and Ed Draper all confirm George Walls' kidnapping activities, pointing to his significant wealth, which came from an undisclosed source.

[34]*American Republican* (West Chester): November 21, 1854.

[35]See the *Jeffersonian:* November 10, 1860 as well as issues throughout the previous decade.

[36]*Jeffersonian:* December 15, 1860.

[37]*American Republican* (West Chester): October 22, 1850.

[38]*Jeffersonian:* November 3, 1860.

[39]John Hope Franklin, *From Slavery to Freedom: A History of Negro Americans* (New York: Afred A. Knopf, Inc., 1980, fifth edition), 201-202.

THE LIBERATOR

Is a periodical, published every Saturday morning, in Boston, Massachusetts, by Wm. Lloyd Garrison and Isaac Knapp, and devoted to the Abolition of Slavery, and the Cause of the Free People of Color. Price $2 per annum, payable in advance. Subscriptions gratefully received.

4.
Pushing *the* Line

Those who promoted the abolition of slavery composed another substantial part of Chester County's antebellum population. Most advocated gradual emancipation by seeking to convince individual slaveholders that slavery was a sin and personal repentance could only come with manumitting those they held in bondage. Some joined the American Colonization Society, founded in 1816, which sent a small number of "free people of color to Liberia on the west coast of Africa."[1] In this way, they could give a personal witness against slavery, offer a compromise to slaveholders by promoting a gradual approach, and not have to address the widespread fear of assimilating former slaves into white society.

Figure 19, Catalog 6: **William Lloyd Garrison** (1805-1879), a radical abolitionist and editor of the anti-slavery newspaper, *The Liberator.*

With the publication of William Lloyd Garrison's abolitionist newspaper, *The Liberator,* in 1831, however, there were those whites who began to seriously consider a more radical approach that called for the immediate and total abolition of slavery. Garrison opposed the moderation and gradualism of the colonizationists with a zeal that bordered on fanaticism.[2] "I am aware that many object to the severity of my language, but is there not cause for severity?" he asked his readers in the first issue of *The Liberator.* "I *will* be as harsh as truth, and as uncompromising as justice. On this subject, I do not wish to think, or speak, or write with moderation. No! No! Tell a man whose house is on fire to give a moderate alarm; tell him to moderately rescue his wife from the hands of the ravisher; tell the mother to gradually extricate her babe from the fire into which it has fallen - but urge me not to use moderation in a cause like abolitionism. I am in earnest - I will not equivocate - I will not excuse - I will not retreat a single inch - AND I WILL BE HEARD."[3] Two years later, Garrison and sixty-two others established the American Anti-Slavery Society, calling for the immediate and total abolition of slavery.[4]

Disagreements among abolitionists over tactics heightened ideological differences and resulted in a splintered movement throughout the United States. In Chester County, abolitionists sided with either the Colonization Society, or the county's Anti-Slavery Society, and it was not uncommon for each group to express its displeasure with the other. In 1830, the Chester County Colonization Society, under the direction of its president, Dr. William Darlington of West Chester, resolved to "obtain subscriptions and contributions in aid of the expenses of the expedition to Liberia, recently undertaken by the Pennsylvania Colonization Society." Applauding the success of colonization, which in "scarcely ten years" has relocated "upwards of 1,400 inhabitants at the Colony of Liberia," Darlington apologized for the fact that the Chester County Society had, up to that time, not raised more than $257.25 for the cause. He attributed the failure to the "jealousies of some of the more sanguine friends of abolition."[5] The Chester County Anti-Slavery Society, on the other hand, believed "it right to operate against slavery through the ballot box," realizing that it "cannot reasonably expect our

Figure 20: **Dr. William Darlington of West Chester was a champion of colonization (sketch by Dane Tilghman)**

profession of attachment to the principles of liberty to be believed" by those who advocate colonization.[6]

The ideological and tactical differences between these two groups reflect the lack of consensus that existed among Chester County's abolitionists during the antebellum period. Some chose to involve themselves in the "Free Produce" movement, a boycott of slave-made products. Others promoted colonization, and, still others advocated political action through the host of anti-slavery societies that existed in the region. While they may have disagreed on the proper approach, the abolitionists, collectively, heightened public awareness of the evils of slavery. In so doing, they "pushed the line" of slavery past the accepted moral conventions of the time that condoned the peculiar institution. More important, their efforts were carried out within the limits of the civil law.

At the same time, white abolitionists tended to keep a social distance from the free black people who joined their anti-slavery organizations. Fear of assimilation, or worse, miscegenation prevented a closer relationship. Thus, while white abolitionists might have been progressive enough to challenge the moral conventions of an antebellum society that condoned slavery, their inability to transcend the racism of that society inevitably defined them as products of it. Individual members of the Religious Society of Friends, commonly called "Quakers," were not only among the most active abolitionists, but also reflected this moral ambivalence.

Inspired by a theological belief of the presence in each person of a divine spark, Quakers reasoned that if God made His presence available to each person then, in His eyes, all human beings were of equal value, regardless of race, sex, or creed. This so-called "Inner Light" doctrine and the testimony on equality it inspired, often placed Friends well ahead of other American churches in acknowledging the evils of slavery. As early as 1688, a small group of

Figure 22, Catalog 27: GOSHEN FRIENDS MEETING, SHOWN HERE IN 1889, WAS THE FIRST QUAKER MEETING IN CHESTER COUNTY TO FREE THEIR SLAVES AFTER PHILADELPHIA YEARLY MEETING ADOPTED A POLICY, IN 1776, TO DISOWN ALL SLAVEHOLDING MEMBERS.

Figure 21: BENJAMIN LAY, A HUNCHED-BACK DWARF, USED DIRECT CONFRONTATION TO CONVINCE QUAKER SLAVEHOLDERS OF THE EVILS OF SLAVEHOLDING. (COURTESY OF FRIENDS HISTORICAL LIBRARY, SWARTHMORE COLLEGE)

Friends in Germantown, near Philadelphia, challenged the peculiar institution by urging the slaveholders in their church to "stand against" the practice of "bring[ing] men [to this country] or to rob and sell them against their will."[7]

The Society of Friends, however, could not bring themselves to a complete realization of the testimony, especially when their governing body, Philadelphia Yearly Meeting, was controlled by members whose affluence depended on slave labor and the slave trade. Consequently, individual members served to plant the seed for abolitionism within the Society of Friends. Benjamin Lay, for example, was among the most instrumental of these early Quaker abolitionists.

A hunched-back dwarf, Lay earnestly believed that God had selected him as an instrument to end slavery within the Society of Friends and refused to wait for Quakers to achieve consensus on the matter. His method of direct confrontation was based on a desire to show Friends that they committed spiritual and physical violence by holding slaves. In one of his most shocking demonstrations, Lay went before Philadelphia Yearly Meeting in 1738 and plunged a sword into a hollowed out book that resembled a Bible and contained a bladder of red pokeberry juice. Splattering those sitting nearby with "blood," Lay accused the slaveholding Quaker elders of hypocrisy. Predictably, the "blood and bladder" prank resulted in Lay's disownment from the Society of Friends.[8]

A less impassioned, but every bit as passionate Quaker abolitionist was John Woolman, whose work, *Some Considerations on the Keeping of Negroes* (1754) aroused the moral conscience of Philadelphia Yearly Meeting. Appealing to the Christian sympathies of his readers, Woolman reminded them that "to deprive a fellow creature of the sweetness of freedom is a contradiction to true religion itself." If, however, one should "exercise righteousness and loving-kindness towards all men," then there is "a good foundation to hope that the blessing of God will sweeten his treasures during this life and his memory will be savory when entered into rest."[9] By focusing on the temporal as well as spiritual welfare of the owner, rather than the demoralization of the slave, Woolman made slavery the catalyst of a spiritual reformation among Friends. That reformation emphasized the need within Philadelphia Yearly Meeting, the governing body of Friends in southeastern Pennsylvania, to purify itself by requiring all members to return to a primitive simplicity in behavior and lifestyle.

Friends became more insistent that their children not mix with non-Quakers at school, preferring a more guarded education. Marriage outside of the Society of Friends was also discouraged and often resulted in disownment from the monthly meeting. Members were strenuously urged to rid themselves of "vain customs of the world" such as music, theater and art. Swift and sometimes severe disciplinary action was taken against wayward members who deviated from Quaker practice.[10] As part of this spiritual reformation, the Yearly Meeting took a definite step against slavery by declaring its "uneasiness and disunity with the importation and purchasing of Negro and other slaves." "To live in ease and plenty by the toil of those whom violence and cruelty have put in our power," stated the Yearly Meeting leadership, "is not consistent with both Christianity and common justice." The minute concluded with an appeal to Friends to make the case of the Africans "our own and consider what we should think, and what we should feel, were we in their circumstances."[11] Not until 1758, however, did the Yearly Meeting direct its constituent monthly meetings to eliminate from membership all those who continued to buy or sell slaves and, through visiting committees, to persuade owners to free the blacks they already owned.[12]

Enforcement of the 1758 discipline on the buying and selling of slaves widely varied among the meetings of Chester County. Of the county's eight monthly meetings, only Goshen dealt with offenders before 1760. At the other extreme was Uwchlan, which refused to hear any case before 1771. All the other monthly meetings heard at least two cases between 1760 and 1770. Of the 30 cases that were heard, only 6 resulted in disownment or partial disownment, which meant being banned from business meetings. Goshen and Concord dealt most consistently with offenders, but even they tended to treat them leniently. Overseers would report the offense to the monthly meeting which, in turn, assigned Friends to visit with them and convince the offender of the evils of the slave trade. Offenders were then expected to admit their mistakes and promise not to repeat them. Most often an offender explained that they were unaware of the change in the Yearly Meeting's discipline and promised to treat their black slaves well and educate them in the Christian religion.[13]

In 1764, Philadelphia Yearly Meeting followed up on the 1758 minute by instructing the monthly meetings to "take more care in dealing with offenders," and if they refused to do so, warned that they would "send representatives to supervise their meetings."[14] By 1776 growing abolitionist sentiment within the Society of Friends and the growing colonial fervor towards political independence from Great Britain convinced the Yearly Meeting to take the final step and direct all the monthly and quarterly meetings to disown from membership those who refused to free their slaves and to record the manumissions of all those slaves who had been freed.[15]

What had begun in 1688 as a moral protest by a small group of Quakers had, by 1776, become a matter of spiritual integrity for Philadelphia Yearly Meeting itself. Abolitionism, however, was only part of a larger reformation within Philadelphia Yearly Meeting. Friends focused on maintaining the spiritual integrity of their church. Accepting blacks into their fold, or even involving themselves with the continued welfare of those who escaped bondage was, for most Friends, a lesser priority.

Figure 23: **Anthony Benezet.** Quaker abolitionist Anthony Benezet began tutoring black children in his Philadelphia home in 1750, believing that they were every bit as capable of learning as white children. [Taken from John W. Barber, Historical, Poetical and Pictorial American Scenes (New Haven, CT, 1850)]

After 1776, Quaker abolitionist efforts spread to the larger society, but even then, those efforts were largely *individual* commitments which often resulted in the establishment of anti-slavery societies and, at least in one case, educating the children of free blacks. Anthony Benezet, a teacher at the Friends Public School in Philadelphia, began tutoring free blacks in 1750 at his home on Chestnut street.[16] The Overseers of the city's 12 Quaker-run schools were grateful to Benezet for accepting the task of educating blacks, something they did not much relish confronting themselves because of the controversy surrounding the issue. That is probably why they made him an Overseer in 1756.[17] The appointment confirmed the Overseers' support of Benezet's efforts but did little more. In 1770, when his proposal for the establishment of a Quaker-supported school for free blacks gained general acceptance among them, it was Benezet himself who assumed all of the responsibility for raising money, building a structure, and hiring a teacher. Benezet taught at the school until his death in 1784.[18]

Aside from Benezet's efforts, Quakers did little to improve educational opportunities or the living conditions of African Americans . "They will give us good advice, they will aid in giving partial education - but never beside their own children," said black

Figure 24 - 25, Catalog 40 - 41: **Silk purse & silk handkerchief.** By the 1840s, Chester County's Quakers became adept at marketing the abolitionist cause with such items as this silk purse and this silk handkerchief, which bore the image of the Declaration drafted by the 1833 Anti-Slavery Convention held at Philadelphia.

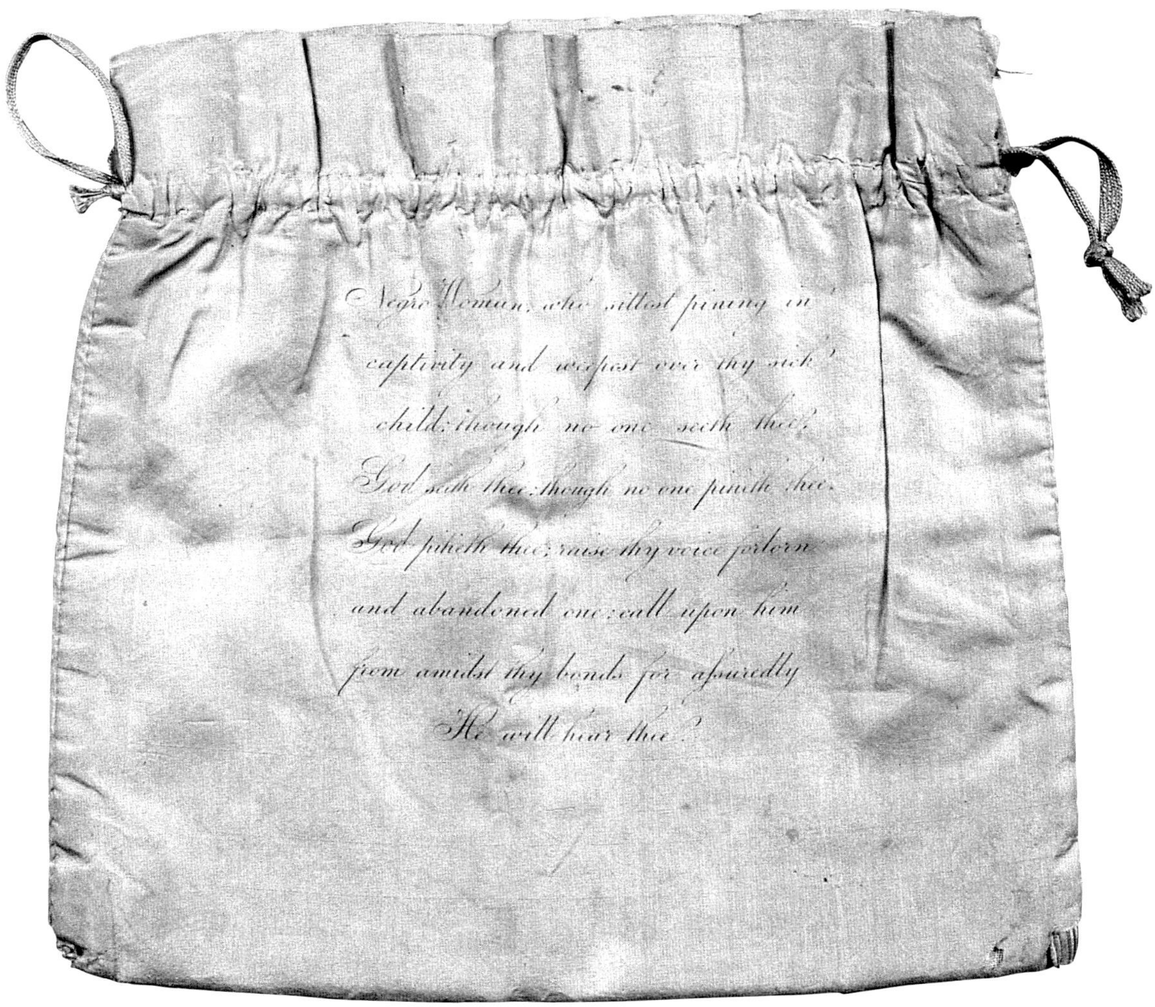

minister Samuel Ringgold Ward of the Quakers in the early 19th century. "Whatever they do for us savors of pity, and it is done at arm's length."[19]

Predictably, Friends discouraged black membership in their meetings. African Americans were welcome to attend the meeting for worship, as long as they sat in the special sections reserved for their race. Full membership, however, was strongly discouraged because of the Quaker fear of assimilation.[20] Those black people who were admitted to membership were scrutinized by the Meeting hierarchy more carefully than a white candidate, and skin color was an important factor in the decision. For example, Abigail Franks, a mulatto woman, applied to Concord Monthly Meeting for membership in July 1781 and Concord promptly sent her application on to the quarterly meeting. Chester Quarterly Meeting, in turn, appointed a committee of Friends to "consider the subject" and also to "inquire more minutely into the disposition, color and circumstance of the individual making application."[21] On February 11, 1782, the committee reported to the quarterly meeting that Abigail's "disposition was worthy of Friends notice and her color appeared not darker than some who are esteemed white."[22] Nevertheless, the quarterly meeting recommended that the case be taken to Philadelphia Yearly Meeting which, in October 1783, advised Concord Meeting that they may "safely consider the application for membership on the same ground as others."[23] Finally, on April 7, 1784—almost four years after she applied for membership—Franks was admitted into the Religious Society of Friends.[24]

Fears of miscegenation resulted in subtle forms of discrimination among Friends well into the nineteenth century. John Chandler, a British Friend who traveled through southeastern Pennsylvania in the 1840s, noted that working-class whites were not the only ones who "harboured a great dislike of their colored fellow-citizens," but also that the "members of our own religious society make no effort to overcome their general prejudice." "They are kind to the colored people by performing many disinterested acts of love and mercy," he wrote,

Figure 26: ABRAHAM SHADD, MARY ANN SHADD'S FATHER, WAS AN ARDENT OPPONENT OF COLONIZATION. (COURTESY OF BUXTON MUSEUM, UNIVERSITY OF WESTERN ONTARIO)

"but still they seem to consider them aliens—as a people who have no right to a possession in the land that gave them birth."[25]

As the nineteenth century progressed, Chester County's white and black abolitionists would keep a respectful distance from each other, socially, but they would also work together in a variety of anti-slavery activities. Among the least controversial of these was the Free Produce movement.

Designed to put pressure on slaveholders, the Free Produce movement was an economic boycott of slave-made products. The ultimate aim was to force slaveowners to give up their slaves in order to survive in a free-produce market. Organized in 1827, the Free Produce Society of Pennsylvania succeeded in placing free labor textiles and foodstuffs on the market as well as promoting the establishment of local organizations. In Chester County, George W. Taylor of New Garden, and Eli Hambleton and Hannah Smith of Hamorton, and Benjamin and Hannah S. Kent of West Grove, operated free produce stores as a way to demonstrate their personal opposition to slavery.[26] Because free-produce goods cost more than slave-made ones, mainly those abolitionists who had the financial means to purchase them were likely to participate in the move-

Figure 27: ASHMUN INSTITUTE. FOUNDED IN 1854 IN LOWER OXFORD, TO TRAIN BLACKS FOR MISSIONARY WORK IN LIBERIA. ORIGINALLY NAMED FOR A BLACK MISSIONARY, JEHUDI ASHMUN, IT LATER CHANGED ITS NAME TO LINCOLN UNIVERSITY IN HONOR OF THE MARTYRED PRESIDENT. (COURTESY OF LANGSTON HUGHES MEMORIAL LIBRARY ARCHIVES, LINCOLN UNIVERSITY)

ment. However, there is some indication that membership in some of the local anti-slavery societies required the purchase of non-slave-made goods. At the annual meeting of the East Fallowfield Anti-Slavery Society in 1837, for example, members passed such a resolution.[27] The following year the Schuylkill Township Anti-Slavery Society did the same.[28] Nevertheless, the Free Produce movement did not achieve the same following as did other forms of anti-slavery activity and, by the 1850s, it was largely a personal witness against slavery by Quakers who did not feel comfortable with more direct action. A more public form of anti-slavery activity was colonization, or the deportation of freed blacks to Africa.

As far back as 1776, Thomas Jefferson proposed a plan for African colonization of blacks. His proposal was passed by the Virginia Assembly in the early 19th century and resulted in the establishment of the American Colonization Society in 1816. Free black people were first sent to the British colony of Sierra Leone, and finally, in 1821, a permanent location was purchased at Monrovia, later the independent Republic of Liberia.[29]

Figure 28, Catalog 35: REVEREND JOHN M. DICKEY. FOUNDER OF THE ASHMUN INSTITUTE AND A SUPPORTER OF COLONIZATION.

The Chester County Colonization Society was founded in 1827 by Dr. William Darlington. Like the earlier American Colonization Society, the organization raised funds to "remove sundry free persons of color" to Liberia because of "the desire to rid ourselves of a population injurious to us, as it must be unpleasant to themselves."[30] Colonizationists cut across denominational boundaries. In southern

Chester County, for example, Quakers Mahlon Brosius, Charles Hambleton, Elizabeth Kent, and Elliot Cresson joined with John Miller Dickey, a pastor of the Oxford Presbyterian Church to advocate the expatriation for both slaves and free blacks to Africa.[31]

By the 1820s, most free blacks challenged the colonizationists. Abraham Shadd, a free black shoemaker of West Chester, played an important role in shaping the abolitionist rhetoric in opposition to colonization. Along with his daughter, Mary Ann, he attended colonization meetings in Philadelphia and Wilmington, Delaware, as well as in Chester County, and argued that the movement was a violation of black Americans' constitutional rights. "We are constrained to believe that the welfare of the people of color is but a secondary consideration with those engaged in the colonization project," stated Shadd. "We are natives of the United States. We have our attachments to the soil, and we feel that we have rights in common with other Americans." Instead of colonization, Shadd demanded "amalgamation," and focused on black peoples' need for education.[32]

As black opposition grew, the colonizationists forged ahead with their plans for black resettlement. In 1854, Dickey founded the Ashmun Institute "for the scientific, classical and theological education of colored youth of the male sex," with the purpose of training blacks to become missionaries to Africa.[33] Named for Jehudi Ashmun, a black missionary who dedicated himself to the interests of American colonization in Liberia, the Institute quickly became a community project.[34] The free blacks of nearby Hinsonville helped to construct buildings, attended classes, and donated their time and money. Among the first graduates were Samuel Glasgow and James and Thomas Amos. Ordained as Presbyterian ministers, the Amos brothers immediately set sail for Liberia to serve as missionaries. Glasgow followed in 1859, to help recruit students for Ashmun. Together the three men helped to

Thou shalt tread upon the lion and adder; the young lion and the dragon shalt thou trample under feet.

DECLARATION OF THE ANTI-SLAVERY CONVENTION.

ASSEMBLED IN PHILADELPHIA, DECEMBER 4, 1833.

Figure 29, Catalog 39: Declaration of the Anti-Slavery Convention, at Philadelphia, December 4, 1833

establish the Presbytery of West Africa, which had strong ties to the Presbyterian synods of New York and Pennsylvania.[35]

Colonization offered whites a legal means of promoting anti-slavery activity without fearing the consequences of assimilation. Operating on the assumption that private manumission was the only safe approach, white colonizationists advocated resettlement in order to avoid social turmoil. While they genuinely hated slavery, they believed that the two races could never coexist without it.

At the same time, there were those free black people who were attracted to colonization because of the daily racism they encountered in northern society or the fear of being kidnapped and sold into bondage. "American blacks are weak when compared with whites, numerically, and face a torrent of opposition," wrote Thomas Amos to John Dickey, shortly after his arrival in Liberia. "Why not advise them to seek a new home where they can be happy and enjoy all the rights of Christian freemen?"[36]

Despite the efforts of colonizationists like Amos and Dickey, the movement waned in the 1850s with a total of only 12,000 blacks colonized by 1860.[37] More effective was the Pennsylvania Anti-Slavery Society and its many local affiliates.

Founded in Philadelphia by Benjamin Franklin in 1787, the Pennsylvania Anti-Slavery Society [PASS] was the very first organization in America dedicated to abolitionism. During its early years, the society devoted itself to sending anti-slavery petitions to Congress and protecting free blacks from kidnappers. Among the earliest members were Chester County Quakers, including: Richard Barnard, Jr., Edward Bonsall, William Gibbons, Enoch Lewis, Emmor Kimber, John Meredith, Samuel Painter, Jr., and Thomas Vickers.[38] When the PASS was re-organized at Harrisburg in 1837, Hamorton's Dr. Bartholomew Fussell was elected Vice-President and 26 of the delegates appointed were also from Chester County, including, Edward Bartlett, Henry Fleming, Nathan and David Evans, Emmor Kimber, Samuel Painter, and Aaron and Paxson Vickers. By that time, the PASS had also established an impressive track record for buying the freedom of slaves, assisting and protecting free blacks, establishing Negro schools, lobbying both the state and federal legislatures on behalf of the abolitionist cause, and nurturing other abolitionist societies within Pennsylvania's boundaries. Because of the prominence of Chester Countians in the Society, many of the annual meetings were held at West Chester's Horticultural Hall.[39]

In 1833, Fussell joined Garrison and Lewis Tappan to establish the American Anti-Slavery Society [AASS]. Members came from nine states, including Pennsylvania. The founding of this organization marked the beginning of a more aggressive abolitionist movement. The AASS called for the immediate and total abolition of slavery, without any compensation to slaveholders for their loss. Like the earlier Pennsylvania Anti-Slavery Society, the AASS brought anti-slavery petitions before Congress and published abolitionist newspapers.[40] It also spawned many affiliated organizations in Chester County.

Unlike the Chester County Abolitionist Society (founded in 1823) whose methods were non-combative, these new affiliated societies were more radical in their approach to abolitionism. The Clarkson Anti-Slavery Society in the southwest part of the county, for example, viewed one of its major responsibilities as attacking the local colonization society. Criticizing the colonizationists' attempt to impose a head tax on each "colored male" plus additional state funds to "finance the passage of free Negroes to Liberia," the Clarkson Society, in 1840, charged the colonizationists with hypocrisy. While they "pretended compassion" for the slave, they were in fact "as bad as the slaveholders," having nothing but "feelings of dislike or antipathy towards the colored race."[41]

The Ercildoun, Bradford and Lundy Union Anti-Slavery societies took their crusade to the state legislature. Throughout the 1840s, a flood of petitions came from all three organizations lobbying Harrisburg to "remonstrate with the southern legislatures against the continued support of slavery."[42] Considering the many anti-slavery officials Chester County elected to the state legislature, those petitions were given a fair hearing. Among the most prominent anti-slavery state representatives were: Jesse C. Dickey, Henry S. Evans, Abraham R. McIlvaine, Elijah F. Pennypacker, Paxson Vickers, and William T. Shafer.[43]

But even the anti-slavery societies were divided over the degree of political action. The Ercildoun, Bradford and Clarkson anti-slavery societies, for example, favored the establishment of a political party, believing that slavery was a political issue and that the existing parties were not moving fast enough or very effectively on abolition. On the other hand, the Lundy Union, Chester County and East Fallowfield anti-slavery societies believed that slavery was a moral, if not religious, issue. They argued that abolitionists should support those anti-slavery candidates in the existing parties, men like Chester County's own Jesse Dickey, William Everhart and John Hickman, who were already serving in Congress.[44]

Figure 30: **Abraham Lincoln.** Chester County's Republican party can be traced to 1855 when a gathering of former Whigs passed a resolution denouncing the Missouri Compromise. Five years later, the county would help to secure the presidency for Republican candidate Abraham Lincoln. (Courtesy of Library of Congress)

Although an anti-slavery "Liberty Party" was organized in 1839, it did not enjoy much success in subsequent elections and was replaced, in 1848, by a new, "Free Soil Party." Like its predecessor, the Free Soilers lost both the '48 and '52 presidential elections by overwhelming majorities. Not until 1855, when anti-slavery reformers joined forces with the remnants of the Whig and Know Nothing parties to form a new "Republican" party, did they realize success.

In Chester County, the first meeting of the Republicans was held at West Chester on August 11, 1855. The gathering passed a resolution denouncing the repeal of the Missouri Compromise and the lack of presidential action in Bleeding Kansas.[45] Predictably, the local Democrats attacked the Republicans for being a "sectional party," bent on "splitting the union with their anti-slavery views."[46] In the Election of 1856, Chester County supported the Republican candidate John C. Frémont for the presidency, who was soundly defeated by Democrat James Buchanan at both the state and national levels.[47] In the 1858, mid-term elections, however, the Republicans received solid support from Chester County as well as from the state of Pennsylvania, setting the stage for Abraham Lincoln's presidential victory in 1860.[48]

To be sure, the Republican Party's success cannot be attributed to the abolitionist movement in Chester County, or anywhere else for that matter. Abolitionism attracted only a small minority of the population. However, the rhetoric they used was sufficiently offensive to alienate others, some of whom might have otherwise been supporters of their cause. Predictably, Chester County witnessed several incidents of anti-abolitionist confrontation.

In March 1837, for example, an anti-slavery meeting at the West Chester Courthouse was interrupted when a "cayenne pepper was put in the stove." Windows were open for ventilation, but shortly after, "eggs were thrown in by persons outside," and the "window over the door, smashed to pieces."[49] The following month, an anti-abolitionist meeting was held at the Methodist Episcopal Church in West Chester so that the "odious doctrines, unwarrantable assumptions and indiscreet course of abolitionists should be repudiated in the most emphatic and decided terms."[50] While the attenders agreed that slavery was indeed an "evil institution," they also insisted that "it can only be removed by a union of the hearts and hands of the ablest people in the country," and "not by insulting southerners, using force, or assuming airs of superiority over others."[51] Nor was the conflict limited to West Chester.

In 1844, Nathan Evans of the Lundy Union Anti-Slavery Society invited Charles Burleigh, the black editor of the abolitionist newspaper *Pennsylvania Freeman,* to speak at the Willistown School House. Shortly after Burleigh began his talk, a hornet's nest was tossed in through an open window and the gathering was forced to reconvene elsewhere.[52] Another popular speaker, Elijah F. Pennypacker of the Schuylkill Township Anti-Slavery Society in Phoenixville, was so candid about the sinfulness of those who condoned slavery that he was eldered by the local Quaker meeting, which considered him as a "Friend to be endured, rather than endorsed."[53]

There was even conflict between black and white people within the same anti-slavery society. At a September 1856 gathering at West Chester, fist fights broke out between white and black abolitionists when it was suggested that the black man was intellectually inferior.[54] Similarly, at a meeting of the Pennsylvania Anti-Slavery Society held at Kennett in 1860, Robert Purvis, a well-educated mulatto, lashed out at the sanctimonious statements of one white attender who insisted that he had "never known prejudice against color" and the fact that he had "eaten and slept in the same bed with black men" was the "severest test of a man's anti-slavery faith."[55]

"I utterly repudiate the idea that social intimacy with colored men is a test of anti-slavery character," said Purvis, as he began his heated rebuttal. "Sir, what has eating, or sleeping with a man to do with the question of human rights? This, sir, is a novel anti-slavery doctrine." Purvis went on to argue that blacks asked no favors of any man or class, and that the issue was not so much a matter of color as principle. "Social intercourse is regulated by irreversible social laws," he insisted. "Every man will find his level. Gentlemen will associate with gentlemen; vulgarity will find its natural place, and true refinement will be respected without regard of color. This is what the glorious anti-slavery enterprise should be teaching the people of this country."[56] Realizing that free blacks in the North had long labored for the franchise with little success, Purvis still continued to argue for black citizenship at abolitionist meetings in the future.[57]

Throughout the antebellum period, abolitionist activity created conflict as well as an important national debate over the issues of slavery and race relations. While many white people viewed slavery as a moral blot on American society, black people were also concerned with the effects of slavery and discrimination on their people. Furthermore, white abolitionists tended to see slavery as absolute moral opposites; a person was either slave or free. Blacks, on the other hand, knew that there were degrees of freedom, that Northern discrimination restricted that freedom, and that there were relative degrees of servitude in the South. Predictably, the Free Produce movement, colonization, and political action were primarily *white* forms of anti-slavery activity. They also represented a progression of involvement and radicalism, rather than separate categories.

Sometimes the progression reflected a change in personal ideology or even the realization that another approach might be more practical, if not more effective, than a previous involvement. Nor did involvement in any one or combination of these activities preclude the individual's participation in the Underground Railroad, especially for Quakers. Still, more abolitionists were involved in these activities than in the Underground Railroad because they were conducted within the limits of the civil law. It was safe, rarely jeopardizing one's own personal safety or financial welfare.

The vanguard of the anti-slavery movement, then, was not those who purchased free produce, or the colonizationists, or even those who belonged to Chester County's various anti-slavery societies. That distinction belonged to the radical abolitionists who participated in the Underground Railroad.

Endnotes *to* Chapter Four

[1]"Constitution of the Chester County Auxiliary of the American Colonization Society," 1830. Chester County Historical Society. The Chester County Auxiliary of the Colonization Society met annually at the Court House in the borough of West Chester.

[2]See Henry Mayer, *All On Fire: William Lloyd Garrison and the Abolition of Slavery* (New York: St. Martin's Press, 1998) for the most extensive treatment of Garrison's role in the shifting ideologies of abolitionist. Mayer identifies Garrison's religious fervor as the driving force behind his immediatist views, believing that the Boston editor planned to "subvert the social order by coaxing a new order of holiness from what he perceived to be the moral chaos of American life." At the same time, it is important to note that the unconditional abolition of slavery did not originate with Garrison and *The Liberator,* but with an English Quaker, Elizabeth Heydrick. Heydrick's 1824 pamphlet, *Immediate, Not Gradual Abolition,* enjoyed several reprintings in the United States. The eloquence of her argument "inspired Garrison's soul." [See Mayer, *All On Fire,* 70].

[3]William Lloyd Garrison, *The Liberator:* January 1, 1831.

[4]Mayer, *All On Fire,* 173-77.

[5]Dr. William Darlington, "Report of the Chester County Colonization Society," *Village Record:* February 10, 1830.

[6]See "A Call For a Convention of Voting Abolitionists," *American Republican:* April 30, 1844; and "Proceedings of Abolition Convention," *American Republican:* May 21, 1844.

[7]Francis Daniel Pastorius, "Germantown Protest, 1688" quoted in Thomas E. Drake, *Quakers and Slavery in America* (New Haven: Yale University Press, 1950).

[8]Roberts Vaux, *Memoirs of the Lives of Benjamin Lay and Ralph Sandiford: Two of the Earliest Public Advocates for the Emancipation of the Enslaved Africans* (Philadelphia, 1815), 17, 25-28; and William C. Kashatus, "The Friends Fight for Freedom," *Pennsylvania Heritage* (Spring 1988): 4-7.

[9]John Woolman, "Some Considerations on the Keeping of Negroes" (1754) in *The Journal and Major Essays of John Woolman,* edited by Philips P. Moulton (New York: Oxford, 1971), 198-209.

[10]Jack Marietta, *The Reformation of American Quakerism, 1748-1783* (Philadelphia: University of Pennsylvania Press, 1984). Marietta argues that Philadelphia Yearly Meeting initiated a spiritual reformation in the 1750s to purge itself of the worldliness of its members. Quakers not only resigned from Pennsylvania government enmasse, but adopted the black, drab white and plain grey clothing as "peculiar badges" of their faith. The ultimate result of this transformation, however, was the elimination of slavery among members.

[11]*Philadelphia Yearly Meeting* (hereafter, "PYM") Minutes: 1754.

[12]*PYM Minutes:* 1758.

[13]Soderlund, *Quakers and Slavery,* 90-95.

[14]*PYM Minutes:* 1764.

[15]*PYM Minutes:* 1776.

[16]William Penn Charter School, *Minutes of the Board of Overseers of the Friends Public School:* 12-27-1756. Quaker Collection, Haverford College Library.

[17]Nash, *Forging Freedom,* 29.

[18]Anthony Benezet, *A Short Account of that Part of Africa Inhabited by the Negroes* (Philadelphia, 1762; *Some Historical Account of Guinea* (Philadelphia, 1771); *Short Observations on Slavery* (Philadelphia, 1781); and Nancy Hornick, "Anthony Benezet and the African's School: Toward a Theory of Full Equality," *Pennsylvania Magazine of History and Biography,* 99 (1975), 388-421.

[19]Samuel Ringgold Ward, *Autobiography of a Fugitive Negro* (1855) (New York: Arno Press, 1968 reprint), 42.

[20]Henry J. Cadbury, "Negro Membership in the Society of Friends," *Journal of Negro History,* 21 (1936): 151-213.

[21]Birmingham Friends Meeting, *250 Years of Quakerism at Birmingham, 1690-1940* (West Chester, PA, 1940), 21-22.

[22]*Ibid.,* 22.

[23]*Philadelphia Yearly Meeting Minutes:* 10-1-1783.

[24]Birmingham Friends Meeting, *250 Years of Quakerism,* 23; and Herbert Aptheker, "The Quakers and Negro Slavery," *Journal of Negro History* XXV (July 1940): 356.

[25]John Chandler, "Letters on America, No. 2" *The British Friend* (Glasgow) No. 1 (1843): 55.

[26]*Proceedings of the Lundy Union Anti-Slavery Society:* February 5, 1842. Chester County Historical Society.

[27]David Evans, *Journal,* 63.

[28]*Proceedings of the Schuylkill Township Anti-Slavery Society:* September 21, 1837. Chester County Historical Society.

[29]Franklin, *From Slavery to Freedom,* 177.

[30]*American Republican:* February 5, 1828.

[31]Bond, *Education for Freedom*, 194-203; and John Bradley, *The Dickey Family and the Growth of Oxford and Hopewell* (Elkton, MD: C & L Printing, 1990), 17.

[32]See Abraham Shadd, quoted in *The Liberator*: September 24, 1831; See also *American Republican*: August 23, 1853; and Jane Rhodes, Mary Ann Shadd Cary: *The Black Press and Protest in the Nineteenth Century* (Bloomington: Indiana University Press, 1998), 10-12.

[33]See *The Foundation of Ashmun Institute* (1853): October 4, 1853. Lincoln University Archives; See also Andrew E. Murray, "The Founding of Lincoln University," *Journal of Presbyterian History* (Winter 1973): 392-410; George B. Carr, *John Miller Dickey, His Life and Times* (Philadelphia: Westminster Press, 1929), 161-62; Bond, *Education for Freedom*, 209-10; and Carter G. Woodson, *The History of the Negro Church* (Washington D.C. Associated Publishers, 1921), 152. An earlier school for the training of free blacks as missionaries was attempted at Parsippanny, New Jersey, but failed.

[34]Bond, *Education for Freedom*, 151; and Paul Russo, "Hinsonville, 1829-1868: A Sketch of a Chester County Afro-American Community," (unpublished manuscript, 1974), 14-16.

[35]*Ibid.*, 488-491.

[36]Thomas Amos to Reverend John M. Dickey, July 11, 1860. Lincoln University Archives.

[37]William C. Patten, "The Anti-Slavery Movement in Chester County" (Master's Thesis, University of Delaware, 1963), 68.

[38]Edward R. Turner, "The First Abolitionist Society in the United States," *Pennsylvania Magazine of History and Biography*, XXXVI, No. 1 (1912): 94-95.

[39]Patten, "Anti-Slavery Movement in Chester County," 43-47.

[40]Still, *Underground Railroad*, 695-96; and C. Peter Ripley, *The Underground Railroad: National Park Service Handbook*. (Washington D.C.: U.S. Department of the Interior / National Park Service, 1998), 62.

[41]*American Republican*: March 10, 1840.

[42]*Pennsylvania Freeman*: December 17, 1840; January 1, 1846; August 16, 1849.

[43]Patten, "Anti-Slavery Movement in Chester County," 62-64.

[44]See *Proceedings of the Lundy Union Anti-Slavery Society*: November 7, 1840, CCHS; *Village Record*: September 26, 1843; *American Republican*: September 10, 1839; and *American Republican*: June 13, 1843.

[45]*Village Record*: August 21, 1855.

[46]*American Republican*: August 21; September 4, 18; and October 16, 1855.

[47]*American Republican*: October 21; November 11, 1856.

[48]*American Republican*: November 13, 1860.

[49]Letter from Townsend Haines to Francis James, March 7, 1837, CCHS

[50]*American Republican*: April 18, 1837.

[51]*American Republican*: April 25, 1837.

[52]*Daily Local*: July 20, 1887.

[53]Still, *Underground Railroad*, 688-90; *Daily Local*: January 5, 1888.

[54]*Jeffersonian*: September 20, 1856.

[55]Reverend H.P. Crozier of Long Island, NY quoted in *Village Record*: October 30, 1860.

[56]Robert Purvis quoted in *ibid*.

[57]Wahl, "Progressive Friends," 287-89.

Faces *of* Abolitionism

Beginning in the early nineteenth century, a secret movement known as the "Underground Railroad" helped black slaves escape from bondage in the South to freedom in the North. Adopting the vocabulary of the railroad, this passage to freedom was made up of a loosely organized network of abolitionists who lived in the Southern border states and in the North and assisted runaways. "Station masters" fed and sheltered runaways in their homes, or "stations," while "conductors" guided fugitives between stations. Four of the most prominent personalities involved on the Eastern Line of the Underground Railroad were Thomas Garrett, Harriet Tubman, William Still and Frederick Douglass.

Figure 31, Catalog 1: Thomas Garrett (1789-1871), Quaker station master from Wilmington, Delaware who assisted more than 2,700 slaves in their flight to freedom through Chester County.

Figure 32, Catalog 2: Harriet Tubman (1821-1913), the most prominent black conductor on the Underground Railroad.

Figure 33, Catalog 3: William Still (1821 - 1902), director of the General Vigilance Committee of Philadelphia, who coordinated the Eastern Line of the Underground Railroad.

Figure 34, Catalog 4: Frederick Douglass (1818-1895), a former slave, became the leading black abolitionist of his time. Publisher of the anti-slaver newspaper, *The North Star*, he was also a gifted orator who often spoke at abolitionist gatherings in Chester County.

Shackles, Chains & Branding Irons

Masters and overseers punished slaves for refusing to obey their wishes, not working hard enough, attempting to escape, and provoking other slaves to rebel.

Those slaves who tried to escape were sometimes forced to wear bells on their arms, neck or head. Some were muzzled. Owners occasionally branded their slaves like cattle to show proof of their ownership.

These shackles, chains and branding iron are powerful reminders of a shameful period in American history when men, women and children were treated as property, their human freedoms denied.

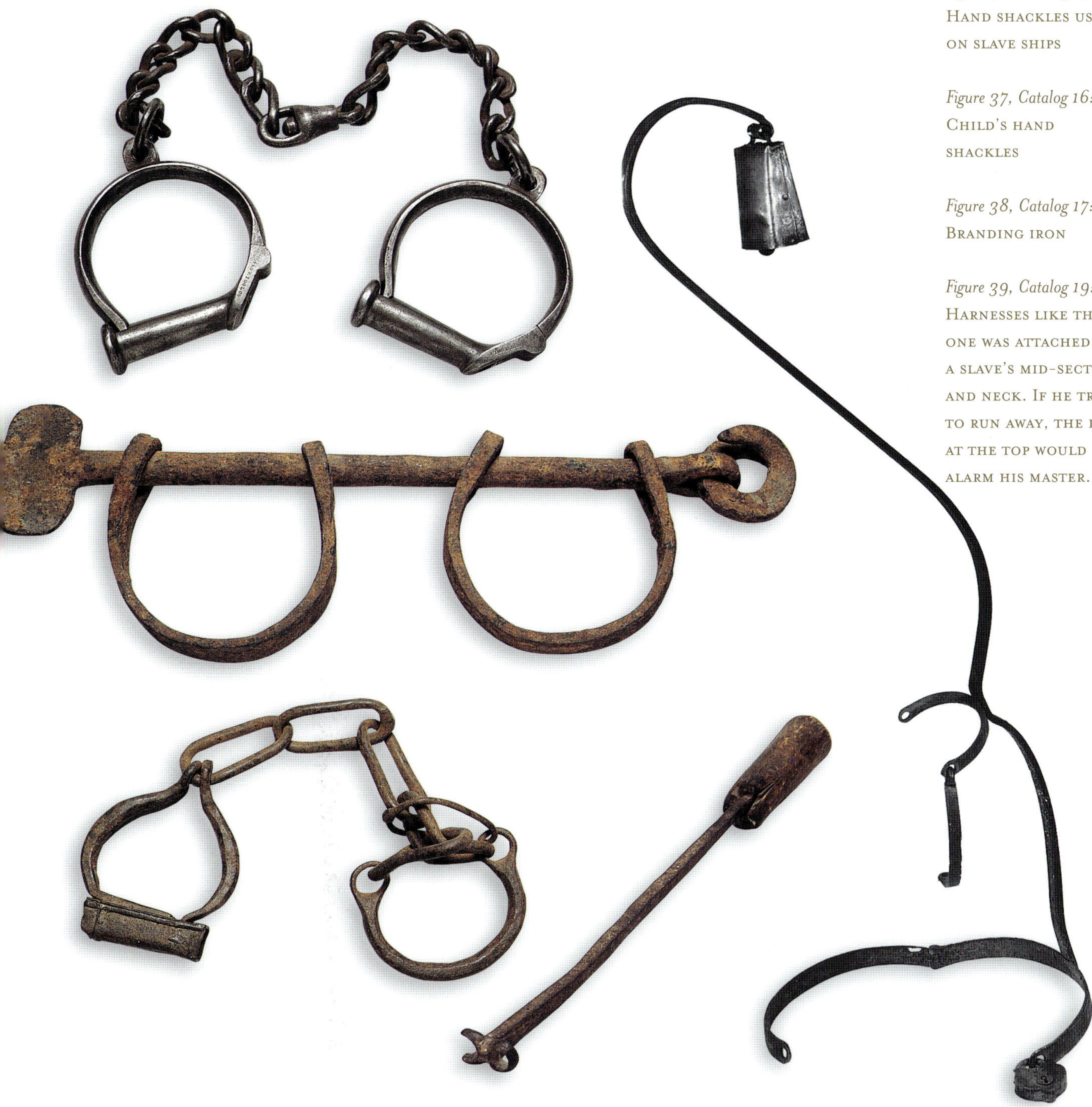

Figure 35, Catalog 15: Adult hand shackles

Figure 36, Catalog 14: Hand shackles used on slave ships

Figure 37, Catalog 16: Child's hand shackles

Figure 38, Catalog 17: Branding iron

Figure 39, Catalog 19: Harnesses like this one was attached to a slave's mid-section and neck. If he tried to run away, the bell at the top would alarm his master.

Reminders *of* Chester County's Anti-Slavery Past

Figure 40, Catalog 31: This daguerreotype of Frederick Douglass was taken about 1848 and given as a gift of friendship to abolitionist Susan B. Anthony. This rare likeness of Douglass is one of the very few images of him as a young man.

The artifacts below once belonged to station masters and other agents on the Eastern Line of the Underground Railroad, which ran through Chester County.

Figure 41, 42, Catalog 56: This silver tea set and tray was presented to Thomas Garrett, a Wilmington station master, on January 11, 1866 from the city's black community for his long-time assistance to fugitive slaves.

Figure 43, Catalog 45: Flowerpot (1838) made by potter John Vickers, a station master who lived in Lionville.

Figure 44, Catalog 62: Corn cutter used as a weapon during the Christiana Resistance

Figure 45, Catalog 26: Bench from Longwood Meeting House, a popular gathering place for Underground Railroad agents near and far.

Chester County Historical Society

A Map and Guide *to the* Underground Railroad

Runaways were among the most intelligent and resourceful slaves. They passed information about methods of escape by word-of-mouth, in stories, and through songs like *"Follow the Drinking Gourd."* Often traveling on foot and by night, fugitives took advantage of the natural protections offered by swamps, bayous, forests and waterways. Those traveling in the East headed to Florida or to such places as Philadelphia, New York, and Boston. Others fled to Ohio, Illinois and Michigan. Some fugitives continued on to Canada, where slavery was outlawed and where officials refused U.S. requests for their return. This map shows the network of Underground Railroad routes that existed in the United States by 1855.

Passage *to* Freedom through Chester County

Chester County was a hotbed of Underground Railroad activity because of its large Quaker population and its proximity to the border states of Delaware and Maryland where slavery was legal. This map, while not a complete index of sites, shows the three major routes used by runaways as well as many of the secondary routes.

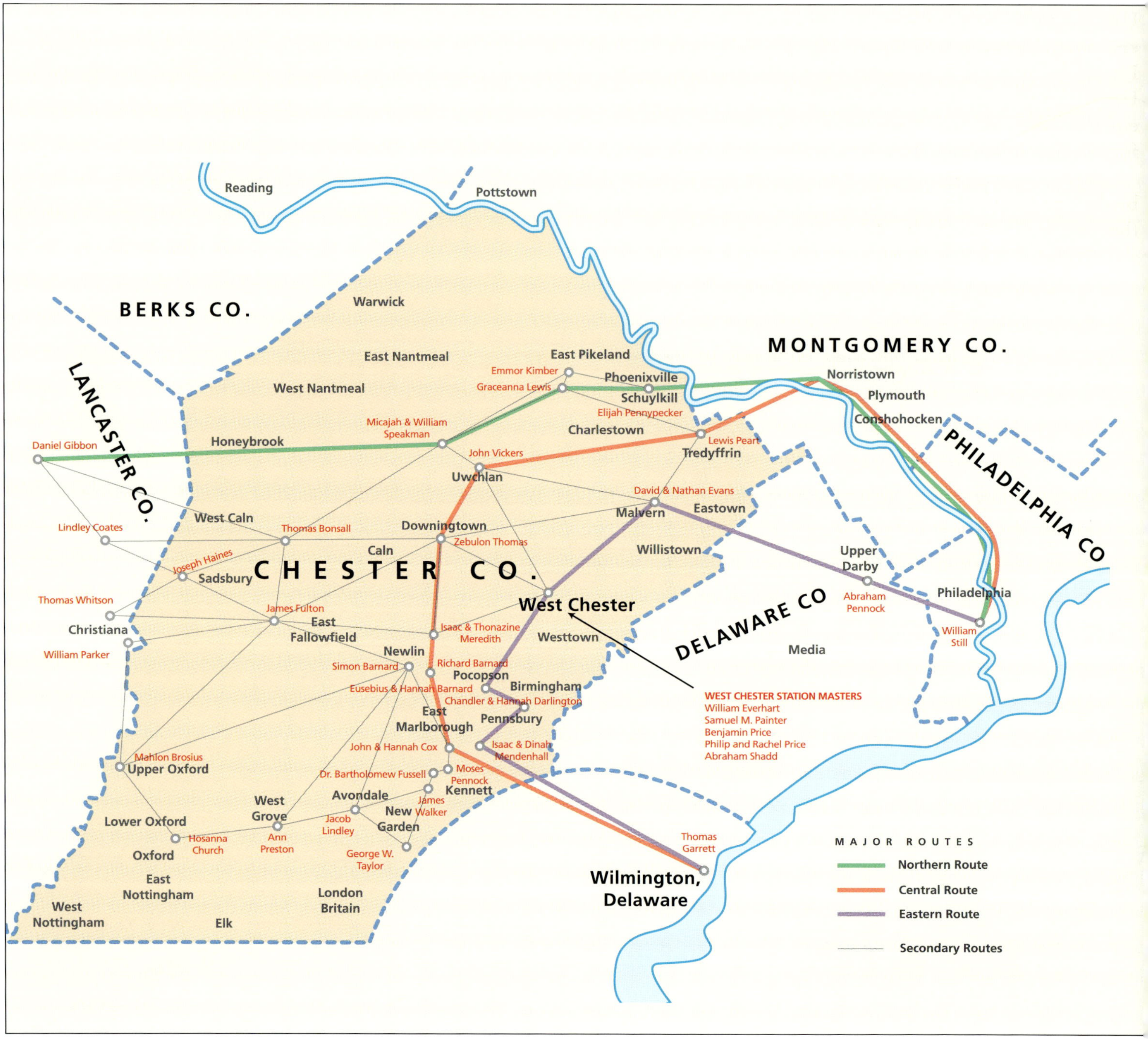

Chester County Historical Society

Breaking *the* Line *of* Slavery

By 1860, there existed a growing rift between the free states and slave states over the future of the nation. Would the United States become a modern country based on free labor or would it continue to depend on slave labor?

When Abraham Lincoln, a Republican and an opponent of slavery, became president in 1861, the South seceded from the Union and it was clear that the issue of slavery would be decided by civil war. Although Lincoln's original aim was to preserve the Union, he soon made Emancipation an equally important goal that eventually transformed the purpose of the war.

Black enthusiasm for the war led many black men, both free and slave, to fight for the Union. At least 60 African Americans from Chester County joined the 54th Massachusetts Colored Infantry, the first regiment to give black people the opportunity to fight. Among their numbers were at least 6 soldiers who were killed on the gallant charge at Fort Wagner in South Carolina. By the end of the Civil War, more than 500 of Chester County's black men had served as other states also established black regiments.

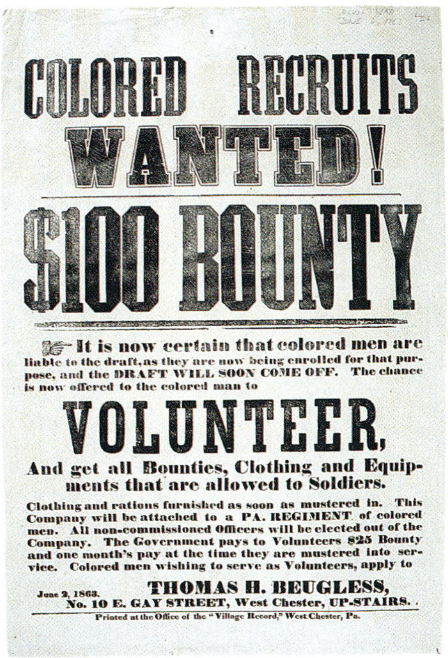

COLORED RECRUITS WANTED!

$100 BOUNTY

It is now certain that colored men are liable to the draft, as they are now being enrolled for that purpose, and the DRAFT WILL SOON COME OFF. The chance is now offered to the colored man to

VOLUNTEER,

And get all Bounties, Clothing and Equipments that are allowed to Soldiers.

Clothing and rations furnished as soon as mustered in. This Company will be attached to a PA. REGIMENT of colored men. All non-commissioned Officers will be elected out of the Company. The Government pays to Volunteers $25 Bounty and one month's pay at the time they are mustered into service. Colored men wishing to serve as Volunteers, apply to

June 2, 1863. THOMAS H. BEUGLESS,
No. 10 E. GAY STREET, West Chester, UP-STAIRS.

Printed at the Office of the "Village Record," West Chester, Pa.

Figure 48, Catalog 80: Badge from 54th Massachusetts, the first black regiment raised during the Civil war

Figure 49, Catalog 79: 1863 handbill advertising for black recruits into the Union army.

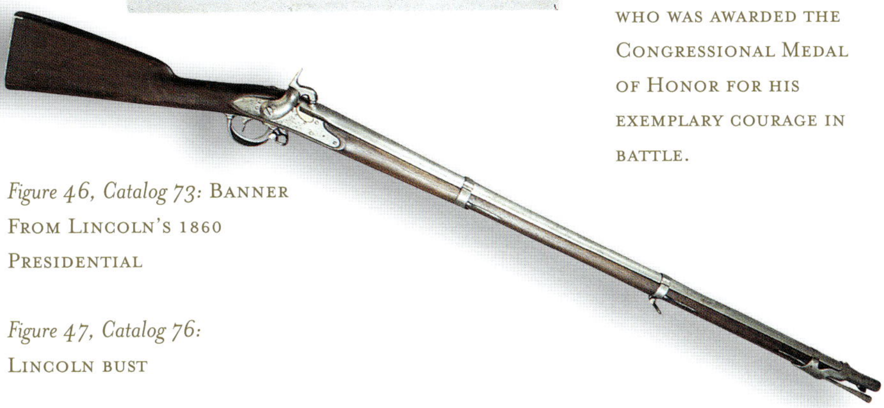

Figure 50, Catalog 83: Rifle belonging to Christian Fleetwood, a graduate of Ashmun Institute who was awarded the Congressional Medal of Honor for his exemplary courage in battle.

Figure 46, Catalog 73: Banner from Lincoln's 1860 Presidential

Figure 47, Catalog 76: Lincoln bust

Chester County Historical Society

Figure 51: By the end of the Civil War, more than 500 of Chester County's black men had fought for the Union as a member of the U.S. Colored Troops. (Courtesy of Library of Congress)

Hope *for a* Divided Legacy *of* Race Relations

Racism, or discrimination based on skin color, came in many forms during the late 1800s and 1900s. Some were subtle. Dolls with distorted Negroid features, for example, were popular in the 1890s, most likely because of their novelty. More hostile forms of racism, however, motivated the activities of the Ku Klux Klan, a white supremacist society that promoted anti-Catholic, anti-Semite and anti-black attitudes throughout the last century. Though not always related to the Klan, lynchings and "separate-but-equal" facilities reinforced the racism that existed in the county long after the Civil War had ended.

These ugly incidents of racism served as a call to action for both white and black Chester Countians to promote a spirit of racial cooperation in the 1900s. Individuals such as Civil Rights leader Bayard Rustin, and artists like Horace Pippin and Ida Jones have answered that call by making valuable contributions to society. Their efforts should inspire us all to continue the dialogue between blacks and whites, as Chester County, like the nation, searches for ways to bridge the racial divide of the past.

Figure 53, Catalog 86: *Mr. Prejudice,* painted by Horace Pippin, a black folk artist from West Chester.

Figures 52, Catalog 88: Mechanical doll with distorted Negroid features

Figure 54, Catalog 91: The Ku Klux Klan was not very popular in Chester County in the twentieth century, but this robe and hood testifies to their existence in the region.

Figure 55, Catalog 84: Elks fraternal club pin

Figure 56, Catalog 98: NAACP Pin, 1977

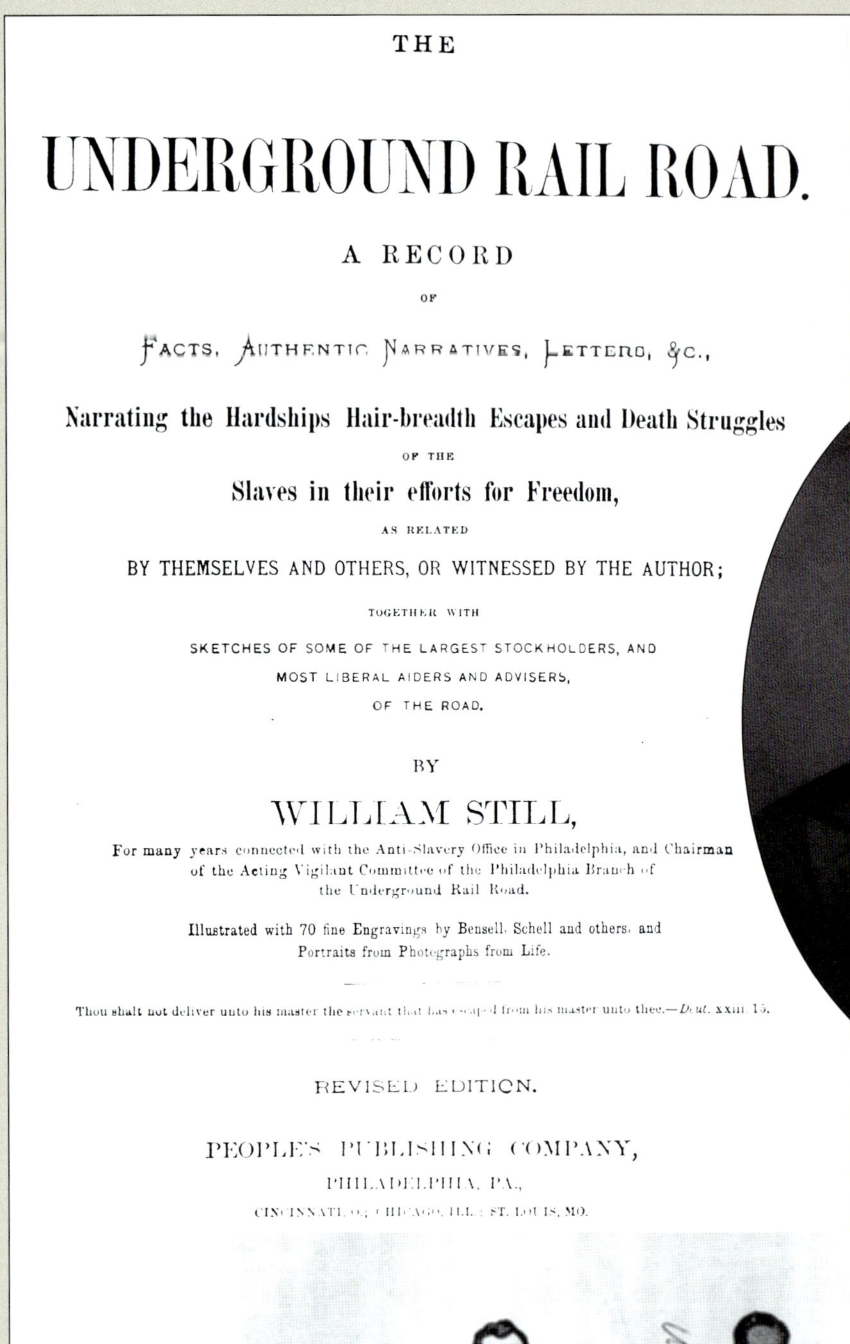

THE

UNDERGROUND RAIL ROAD.

A RECORD

OF

FACTS, AUTHENTIC NARRATIVES, LETTERS, &C.,

Narrating the Hardships Hair-breadth Escapes and Death Struggles

OF THE

Slaves in their efforts for Freedom,

AS RELATED

BY THEMSELVES AND OTHERS, OR WITNESSED BY THE AUTHOR;

TOGETHER WITH

SKETCHES OF SOME OF THE LARGEST STOCKHOLDERS, AND MOST LIBERAL AIDERS AND ADVISERS, OF THE ROAD.

BY

WILLIAM STILL,

For many years connected with the Anti-Slavery Office in Philadelphia, and Chairman of the Acting Vigilant Committee of the Philadelphia Branch of the Underground Rail Road.

Illustrated with 70 fine Engravings by Bensell, Schell and others, and Portraits from Photographs from Life.

Thou shalt not deliver unto his master the servant that has escaped from his master unto thee.—*Deut.* xxiii. 15.

REVISED EDITION.

PEOPLE'S PUBLISHING COMPANY,

PHILADELPHIA, PA.,

CINCINNATI, O.; CHICAGO, ILL.; ST. LOUIS, MO.

Figure 57, Catalog 68: "THE UNDERGROUND RAILROAD." STILL PUBLISHED *THE UNDERGROUND RAILROAD* IN 1872. THE 800-PAGE BOOK CONTINUES TO BE THE MOST ACCURATE ACCOUNT OF THE SECRET PASSAGE TO FREEDOM.

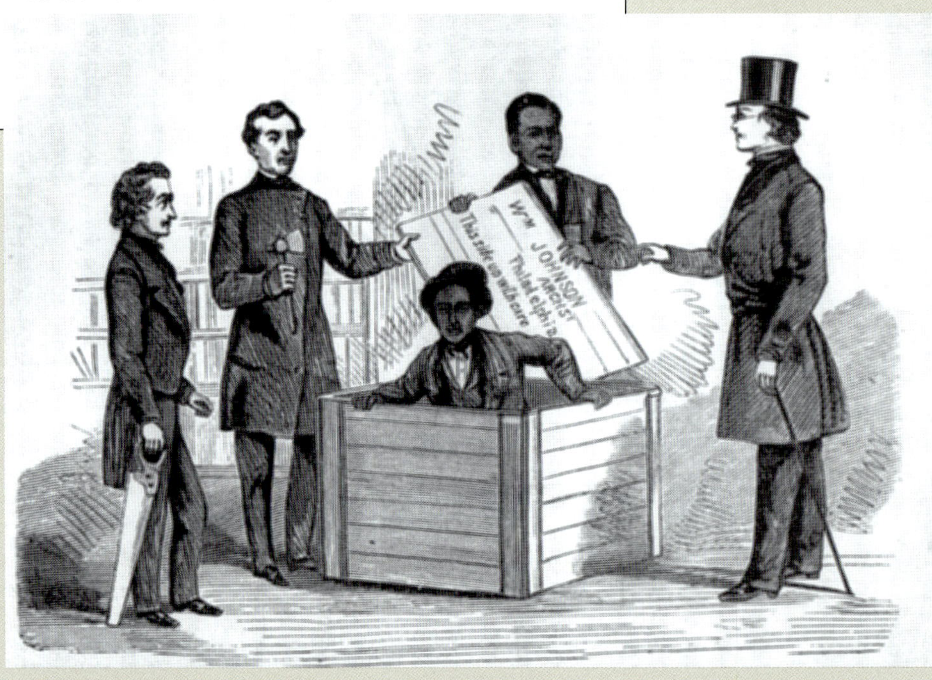

5.

Stepping Over *the* Line

As clerk of the Pennsylvania Anti-Slavery Society's General Vigilance Committee, William Still had grown accustomed to surprises. Not only did the young, free black abolitionist coordinate the Eastern Line of the Underground Railroad by finding shelter as well as an escape route to the North for fugitive slaves, but he recorded their stories of inhumane treatment by brutal owners, painful separations from family, and a passionate desire for freedom. Few of the stories, however, were as remarkable as the one that was about to unfold on this crisp autumn morning.

Figure 58, Catalog 67: **William Still.** William Still recorded the personal histories of runaways who came under his care.

Figure 59, Catalog 69: **Resurrection of Henry "Box" Brown.**

Shortly after opening the doors of his office at 31 North Fifth Street in Philadelphia, Still received a wooden packing crate bound with five hickory hoops. Two feet eight inches deep, two feet wide, and three feet long, the box was from Richmond, Virginia, and marked, "This side up with care."

Suspicious of its content, Still locked the doors, shuttered the windows and gently rapped on the lid of the box, inquiring, "All right?"

An answer came from within: "All right, sir!"

Still cut the hickory hoops and out stepped Henry Brown, a fugitive slave, who, with the aid of a Richmond shoemaker, had himself nailed inside the box and freighted to Philadelphia. After the grueling 26-hour trip, some of which was spent upside-down in the crate, Brown emerged with only a headache and was passed safely on to Boston. News of the remarkable escape caused a sensation in the abolitionist newspapers, as well as increased the demand for Still's services from those wanting to make similar attempts.[1]

Thomas Garrett, a white Quaker abolitionist from Wilmington Delaware, was also in demand. A stocky man who favored a broad-brimmed hat and long, dark waistcoat, Garrett projected a genial disposition, unless he was defending his anti-slavery beliefs. Then he could be outspoken, if not abrasive. Because he was less circumspect in his activities than William Still, Garrett found himself embroiled in a legal dispute of his own making in 1848.

Having been tried and found guilty of harboring a family of fugitive slaves, Garrett was heavily fined and warned by the court "not to meddle with slaves again." Infuriated, more by the warning than the fine, Garrett defiantly replied: "I have assisted over 1,400 runaways in 25 years on their way to the North," remarked the outspoken station master, "and I now consider the penalty imposed upon me as a license for the remainder of my life!"[3]

Judge Roger B. Taney, who presided over the trial, was noticeably shocked by the Quaker station master's beligerance. While he did not believe in slavery, Taney did defend the constitutional right of slaveholders to reclaim their property; a conviction he would uphold nine years later as a Supreme Court Justice in his opinion *Dred Scott v. Sanford.* Just in case Taney doubted his resolve, though, Garrett turned to the spectators and added: "If any of you know of any slave who needs assistance, send him to me, as I now publicly pledge myself to double my diligence and never neglect an opportunity to assist a slave in obtaining his freedom."[4]

Thomas Garrett and William Still were an unlikely pair, differing in temperament, race, creed and age. But their fierce opposition to slavery joined them as co-conspirators on the Eastern Line of the Underground Railroad. Between 1830 and 1863, these two station masters directed some 4,000 runaways to contacts along routes from the upper South to Canada, many passing through Chester County.[5] Both men belonged to a minority of radical abolitionists who violated the civil law in order to carry out what they believed to be the higher law of God in assisting runaway slaves to freedom. Together with other like-minded abolitionists, they "stepped over the line" that defined the legal boundaries of abolitionist activity. More important, their relationship more accurately describes the important interdependence of the white and free black communities in the operation of the Underground Railroad.

Figure 60: Thomas Garrett in old age. (Chester County Historical Society)

Thomas Garrett was born on August 21, 1789 at Upper Darby, Pennsylvania. He was the son of Thomas and Sarah Price Garrett, Quakers whose farmhouse was an active station on the Underground Railroad. Although young Thomas assisted his parents in their abolitionist activities, he did not experience a personal conversion to the cause until 1813.

Returning home after a hard day of farming, Garrett found his family in "sorrow and indignation" at the kidnapping of a free black woman in their employ. He immediately set out to rescue the woman before she could be sold into bondage. During his pursuit, the young Quaker had a spiritual revelation of the "utter sinfulness of slavery." Recovering the woman, he made an unconditional vow to assist slaves in their flight to freedom. Shortly after, Garrett joined the Pennsylvania Anti-Slavery Society and committed himself, wholeheartedly, to the Underground Railroad.[6]

In 1822, Garrett moved to Wilmington, where he became a wealthy merchant and made no secret of his anti-slavery views and activities. Wilmington, which had a population of more than 5,000 and was growing rapidly, was a popular destination for many industrious Quakers who wanted to take advantage of the town's agricultural trade and industry. It was also a hotbed of Underground Railroad activity, being the northernmost town in a slaveholding state. Fugitives from southern Delaware, Maryland and Virginia flocked there in hope of being channeled to freedom.[7] Joining the Delaware Anti-Slavery Society, Garrett and his wife, Rachel Mendenhall, opened their home at 227 Shipley Street as a station on the Underground Railroad.[8] From there he, along with the assistance of free blacks Harry Craige, Isaac Flint, Severen Johnson, Joseph Hamilton, Comegys Munson, and George Wilmer would conduct fugitives across the Mason-Dixon Line into Chester County where he had established contacts with other like-minded Quakers.

Between 1822 and 1863, Thomas Garrett assisted more than 2,320 fugitives on their flight to freedom from his station at Wilmington, Delaware.[9] His station, in particular, was the starting point of the Underground Railroad's eastern line for those slaves coming from Virginia, Maryland and southern Delaware. His outspoken abolitionist views as well as his tireless efforts on behalf of fugitives distinguished him as a leading station master. Neighbors considered his activities "as dangerous to their community and destructive to the Union," yet so impressive was his success in assisting fugitives that Garrett's example served as the inspiration for "Friend Phineas," a character in Harriet Beecher Stowe's famous work, *Uncle Tom's Cabin,* published in 1852.[10] Garrett, however, was only one of many agents who were active on Chester County's Underground Railroad.

Adopting the vocabulary of the railroad to explain their self-appointed duties, these radical abolitionists referred to themselves as "station masters" (those who gave shelter to runaways in their homes, or "stations"), or "conductors" (those who guided fugitives between stations). Less common, but every bit as critical to the success of the Underground Railroad were "stockholders," who contributed the finances needed to feed, clothe and transport fugitives.[11] Agents were both white and black, male and female, slaves and former slaves, and came from a variety of religious and economic backgrounds. Together they organized a loose network of routes that weaved its way through Chester County often leading to Philadelphia where William Still resided.

Generally, the first stop across the Pennsylvania border was the small town of Kennett.[12] Often, Garrett would send runaways to "Oakdale," the Kennett home of a Quaker couple, Isaac and Dinah Mendenhall. This large, square, stone house, along with the adjoining barn and springhouse, sheltered many fugitive slaves until nightfall, when they would be guided on northward. Garrett placed special trust in the Mendenhalls not only because they were Quakers, but because they were also family members, being related to his wife Rachel.[13] But Oakdale was just one of many Kennett area stations.

To avoid predictability, Garrett also sent fugitives to the "Pines", the home of Dr. Bartholomew Fussell, one mile east of Kennett. Fussell was a very respected Quaker physician who had developed a commitment to abolitionism while living in Maryland and observing, first-hand the evils of slavery. There, he taught school during the week and studied medicine at night. Once, when asked to deliver an address before the Medical Society of Baltimore, many of whose members were slaveholders, Fussell denounced

Figure 61, Catalog 49: DINAH MENDENHALL.

Figure 62, Catalog 48: ISAAC MENDENHALL.

Figure 63, Catalog 50: OAKDALE. LOCATED JUST NORTH OF THE MASON-DIXON LINE, OAKDALE WAS THE HOME OF ISAAC AND DINAH MENDENHALL AND ONE OF THE MOST ACTIVE STATIONS ON CHESTER COUNTY'S UNDERGROUND RAILROAD.

the peculiar institution as "the most preposterous and cruel practice" and expressed his hope that one day the "arrogant master and his menial slave will make a truce of friendship and be guided by the same light of Truth."[14] When he moved to Kennett he became involved in a number of reforms, including abolitionism, common schooling, temperance and women's rights.[15] He also opened his house as a station on the Underground Railroad, and established a boarding school for girls, "irrespective of color."[16] "A quiet, discreet, conservative Friend in religious matters," Fussell, according to one fellow abolitionist, was a "radical of the first order in political ones," being a fierce supporter of the Free Soil party.[17] Predictably, he hired fugitives to work on his own farm. According to one legend a fugitive slave by the name of Eliza was paid to keep house while another fugitive, James Washington, was a hired laborer in the fields. Both of these former slaves were, after a time, married in a Quaker wedding ceremony at the doctor's home.[18]

John and Hannah Cox, who also lived near Kennett, provided yet another alternative station. Their home, "Longwood," was on the main road to Philadelphia from points south and west and they eagerly opened it to fugitives, providing food, shelter and clothing before transporting them on to the next station.[19] Inspired by the writings of William Lloyd Garrison, editor of *The Liberator,* and the poetry of John Greenleaf Whittier, the Coxes joined a host of reform movements, including temperance, peace, women's rights and prison reform.[20] But their true passion rested with their work on the Underground Railroad.

According to one legend, the Coxes were preparing to retire for the evening after a hard day's work when they heard a stick being drawn along the boards of their picket fence, a signal that another passenger had arrived at their station. Without hesitation, Hannah made her way downstairs and listened for the caller. Soon a gentle knock followed.

"Who's there?" she inquired.

"Friends," came the whispered reply.

Sliding the heavy bolt which locked the front door, she discovered a family of runaways huddled around a friendly peddler who had guided them from Wilmington.

"One, two, three, four, five friends this time, Jackson," remarked Hannah to the conductor, who was

Figure 64, Catalog 47: John Cox.

Figure 65, Catalog 46: Hannah Cox.

Figure 66, Catalog 53: Cox home. The Coxes, who lived near Kennett, hid many slaves in their four-storey home, which was connected to the barn by an underground tunnel.

clearly pleased by the acknowledgement of his success. "Thee has done well, for there have been slave hunters around this area for three days now. Thank thee. We will take good care of them."

Inviting the family into her home, Hannah quickly closed the door and directed them into the kitchen. Checking that all of the blinds were closed, she lighted a lamp and seated her five charges at the table. A hastily prepared meal of homemade bread, cheese, milk and ham followed. After they finished eating, the father revealed their daring escape from a Maryland plantation, following the grapevine with the North Star as their guide. Somehow they managed to locate the home of Thomas Garrett in Wilmington, who, in turn, placed them in the care of Jackson, a loyal conductor who had assisted the Quaker station master on several occasions.

Hannah then spirited them away to the cellar, where the family would spend the night in the dark bins which once contained coal and wood but were now equipped with rough hewn cots and some homemade quilts.

Figure 67: JAMES WALKER WAS SAID TO HAVE HIDDEN FUGITIVE SLAVES IN THIS HOUSE AT 233 SOUTH UNION STREET, KENNETT SQUARE. THE BUILDING WAS TORN DOWN IN 1989. (BAYARD TAYLOR MEMORIAL LIBRARY, KENNETT SQUARE)

Chester County Historical Society

When morning dawned, Hannah prepared a quick breakfast of hot porridge and took it to the slaves still sleeping in the cellar. Gently awakening them, Hannah fed them and then directed the family through an underground tunnel that connected the house with the neighboring barn. Slowly, carefully, they made their way through the dark passage, Hannah holding a lamp high at one end and John waiting for them in the granary at the other. After they reached him, John helped each member of the family into the back of a dearborn, quickly put the backboard in place and set off for West Chester where he would leave them under the care of yet another station master.[21]

Garrett also depended on other Kennett station masters, including: Moses and Mary Pennock, as well as their son Samuel; John and Lydia Agnew; and Mahlon and Mary Brosius and their sons Edwin and Daniel. Garrett would often dress fugitives in Quaker garb and send them on to these station masters, who came to expect that signature disguise.[22]

One of the most touching incidents involves James Walker, a free black man who lived at 233 South Union Street in Kennett and often assisted Garrett with escaped slaves. A young runaway from Maryland, who had injured his foot leaping from a train near Wilmington, was brought to Walker's house. Walker, with the help of Dr. Isaac D. Johnson and Esther Hayes, nursed the fugitive back to health, though his foot was so severely mangled that the heel and toes had to be amputated. Several weeks had passed and word reached Kennett that the slave's master had learned of his whereabouts. Realizing that the slave had to be moved at once, Walker called on Samuel Pennock, who transported the fugitive one cold, sleeting night.

After twice being refused sanctuary, Pennock finally placed the fugitive with Zebulon Thomas of Downingtown. From there, the runaway gradually made his way to Boston and then to Haiti.

Many years later, Dr. Johnson was visited by a well-dressed black man, who asked if he remembered him. Admitting that he could not, the man introduced himself as "Johnson Hayes Walker," the fugitive that the physician had helped years before. He had taken the name of his three benefactors and had returned to thank them.[23]

Once a fugitive reached Kennett the particular route he took depended largely on circumstance. Since Kennett was like the hub of a wagon with spokes leading in all directions, the fugitives had many choices open to them.[24] Consequently, if there was no space available at a station in West Chester, for example, the route could easily be altered to accommodate that problem. Similarly, alternative stations were often used when a fugitive was being pursued, if only to avoid predictablility. Responsibility for coordinating these routes was largely William Still's.

Still was the youngest of eighteen children of a slave family. His father resettled in New Jersey and became a farmer, after purchasing his own freedon. His mother eventually rejoined her husband after a successful escape. In 1844, Still left his family and moved to Philadelphia. There, with only $5.00 to his name and no friends, he met J. Miller McKim, editor of the abolitionist newspaper, *The Pennsylvania Freeman.* With McKim's assistance, Still learned how to read and write.[25] Three years later, he took a job as clerk with the Pennsylvania Anti-Slavery Society. When the Society organized a Vigilance Committee to assist runaways, in direct opposition to the Fugitive Slave Law of 1850, Still was named the director of the four-person committee.[26]

Shortly after his appointment, a man by the name of Peter Freedman, who had recently purchased his own freedom, paid Still a visit. Freedman was searching for his parents, from whom he had been separated in slavery. As Still listened to the man's story, he came to realize that this was the older brother he had never met, his mother being forced to leave Peter in bondage when she made her escape. "I could see in the face of my new-found brother the likeness of my mother," he would write years later. "My feelings were unutterable."[27]

The incident not only strengthened Still's resolve to help his brother gain freedom for his wife and children still in slavery, but in assisting other fugitives who longed to be reunited with the families. As director of the vigilance committee, he raised funds, corresponded with station masters and conductors along the Eastern route of the Underground Railroad, and coordinated their movements. Relying on the black laboring class, whose members kept a sharp eye out for suspicious whites, Still aided in

Figure 68: RESCUE OF JANE JOHNSON (TAKEN FROM WILLIAM STILL, *THE UNDERGROUND RAILROAD,* 1872)

Chester County Historical Society

Figure 79, Catalog 25: Longwood Meeting House, pictured here in 1865, served as a meeting place for the radical abolitionists of Chester County. Frederick Douglass, John Greenleaf Whittier, and William Lloyd Garrison (shown in this photo with the bouquet of flowers), often spoke at the meetinghouse. Today the building is used by the Chester County Conference & Visitors Bureau, located at the entrance of Longwood Gardens.

December 1, 1850, that the members of Goshen Friends Meeting "received a communication from some colored Methodists desiring the assistance of Friends since the passage of the late fugitive slave law." The meeting "gave evidence of their deep regard for the sufferings of a people whose complexion seemed the only reason for their persecution" and expressed a desire "to provide for their relief."[73] Other meetings proved to be more receptive to anti-slavery reform.

Quakers who left the Kennett and Marlborough Meetings joined with non-Quaker reformers to establish a "Progressive Friends Meeting" at Longwood.[74] On May 22, 1853, the Progressives—a total of 56 Friends—met at the Old Kennett meetinghouse near Hamorton and opened their membership to all those who recognized the "brotherhood of the human family, without regard to sex, color or condition." No issue was "too sacred for examination and discussion," and all issues would be addressed in a manner "free of clerical restraint" that they once felt as members of the Kennett and Marlborough meetings. Among the most pressing issues identified were women's rights, Negro slavery, war, capital punishment and temperance.[75]

While neither side associated the split with the Underground Railroad, many of the Progressive Friends were agents on the clandestine route to freedom. Others were non-Quakers, some of who had already established a prominent national role in abolitionism, including: Sojourner Truth, a former slave and conductor on the Underground Railroad; Lucretia Mott, a leading Philadelphia Quaker reformer; and Thomas M'Clintock, a founder of the Waterloo, New York Progressive Friends.[76]

These radical abolitionists also saw the issues of slavery and womens' rights as inextricably bound. Among their first order of business was to establish a committee that would draft their position on women's rights. This committee consisted of such feminists as: Graceanna Lewis, whose home at Kimberton was an important station on the Underground Railroad, receiving passengers from Wilmington, York, and the southern parts of Chester and Lancaster counties; Hannah Darlington, who convened the first Pennsylvania womens' rights meeting at West Chester in 1852; and Lucretia Mott, who established the Philadelphia Female Anti-Slavery Society in

1833, joining together both white and black women in the cause of abolitionism. For these female reformers, abolitionism garnered not only valuable experience in organizational tactics but a growing awareness of the striking similarities between the oppression of women and that of slaves as they continually faced denials of their right to speak or act politically.[77]

In 1854, the Progressives built their own meetinghouse, which quickly became a center of radical abolitionism. "In dealing with such a sin as slavery, we can adopt no half-way measures," they stated, echoing the immediatist philosophy of Garrison. "The whole truth must be proclaimed, 'without concealment and without compromise.' No Church, no Government, no Constitution, no Union, which requires us to support or sanction such a crime, can have any binding force upon our consciences. We seek not alone to prevent the *extension* of slavery, but to exterminate it from every part of the land."[78] Garrison himself delivered a nearly identical testimony against slavery at Longwood in 1857.[79] In keeping with the Boston abolitionist's tactics, the Progressive Friends contributed to the flood of anti-slavery petitions descending upon Congress in the years before the Civil War. When the Kansas-Nebraska Bill was before Congress on February 7, 1854, Progressive Friends adopted a remonstrance against it, sending it to William Everhart, a member of the House from Chester County and a West Chester station master himself.[80] They also raised funds for anti-slavery societies across the North by holding as well as patronizing anti-slavery fairs.[81] Most noteworthy though, were the open-air mass meetings that were held at Longwood.

On many occasions, Longwood Meeting House was a gathering site for nationally famous leaders of the abolitionist movement, who traveled from all over the country to speak there, including Frederick Douglass, William Lloyd Garrison, Thomas Garrett, John Greenleaf Whittier, Sojourner Truth, and Susan B. Anthony.

Adding to their radical reputation was a common belief among Progressives that once freed, African Americans should enjoy the same liberties as whites. In one testimony after another, Progressive Friends decried the "cruel spirit of caste" which made the "complexion of even free Negroes a badge of social inferiority, exposing them to insult in the steamboat and railcar, and in all places of public resort, not even excepting the church."[82] "Ability" and "effort," they insisted should supercede racial considerations.[83] Accordingly, Progressive Friends demanded equal educational opportunities and the full rights of citizenship for black people, including the ability to vote and hold public office.[84] Just as controversial was the Progressive's involvement on the Underground Railroad. Thomas Whitson stated the philosophy of Progressive Friends most succinctly when, after the passage of the Fugitive Slave Act in 1850, he noted that the "popular notion that the government must be obeyed, whatever its requirements, was all wrong." "Divine Law," he insisted was "superior to acts of Congress," especially if it meant "destroying unjust measures."[85] "Reformers ought to be satisfied to be destructives," echoed Lucretia Mott. "If we are to be 'sharp threshing instruments having teeth we should have some other name than 'reformers.'"[86] Still, the Progressives never officially sponsored the Underground Railroad, realizing that to do so would imperil their own lives as well as those they were attempting to aid.[87]

As virtuous as their efforts were, the station masters and conductors of the Underground Railroad, both black and white, realized that what was needed to effect the immediate abolition of slavery in the country was a much larger movement than they themselves could provide. With the outbreak of the Civil War in 1861 that grand-scale movement had finally arrived.

Endnotes *to* Chapter Five

[1]Still, *Underground Railroad,* 67-72. Henry Brown was not the only runaway who had freighted himself in a packing crate to William Still. Another fugitive was a pregnant woman who was, according to Still, "nearer to death than Henry Box Brown, or any of the other box or chest cases that came under the notice of the committee." [See Still, 632-35] Another was Lear Green, an 18-year-old female who secreted herself in a chest and was stored aboard a steamer. [See Still, 289-92].

[2]Thomas Garrett to *The Blue Hen's Chicken,* June 9, 1848 in McGowan, *Station Master,* 166-68.

[3]Thomas Garrett quoted in *The Blue Hen's Chicken,* June 2, 1848

[4]Garrett to Eliza Wigham, 8-8-1854. Quaker Collection, Haverford College.

[5]Total numbers of fugitives assisted by Garrett and Still were calculated from the statistics given by Charles Blockson, "The Underground Railroad: The Quaker connection," *For Emanicipation and Education: Some Black and Quaker Efforts, 1680-1900.* (Philadelphia: Germantown Historical Society and Awbury Arboretum Association, 1997), 38. Blockson writes that Still and his assistant James Miller McKim "are believed to have helped 300 fugitives a year" during this period. Thomas Garrett kept his own records of fugitives he assisted, which, by November 24, 1863 totaled 2,322 [See Garrett to Samuel May, Jr., 11-24-1863. Boston Public Library].

[6]Still, *Underground Railroad,* 741-44.

[7]McGowan, *Station Master,* 32-38.

[8]Thomas Garrett to Aaron Powell: 4-5-1870 quoted in *The Liberator:* April 1870.

[9]Garrett to Samuel May Jr., 11-24-1863, Boston Public Library.

[10]See Drake, *Friends in Wilmington,* 79; and Martha H. Garrett, Family Recollections (Philadelphia, 1910), 6.

[11]McGowan, *Station Master,* 5.

[12]*Philadelphia Public Ledger:* August 27, 1911.

[13]McGowan, *Station Master,* 43, 115-16; See also *Daily Local News:* December 30, 1882.

[14]Dr. Bartholomew Fussell quoted in Still, *Underground Railroad,* 720-21.

[15]*Journal of Friends Historical Society:* 20:126; and *Friends Intelligencer:* 28: 104.

[16]*Pennsylvania Freeman:* October 9, 1845.

[17]David Evans Diary, 11 mo. 26, 1848. Chester County Historical Society.

[18]Smedley, *History of Underground Railroad in Chester County,* 272.

[19]*Daily Local:* September 15, 1873.

[20]*Philadelphia Public Ledger:* September 25, 1935.

[21]Smedley, *Underground Railroad in Chester County*

[22]Francis C. Taylor, *The Trackless Trail* (Kennett Square, PA, 1976), 20-24, 26-28.

[23]Ibid.; and Walter Grayson, "Historical Sketch of the Underground Railroad," *Kennett Square Centennial Book* (Kennett, PA, 1955), 35.

[24]David Evans, *Journal,* 213-18; Smedley, *Underground Railroad in Chester County,* 100-163.

[25]Still, *Underground Railroad,* vi.

[26]*Ibid.*

[27]Still to J. Miller McKim, August 8, 1850 quoted in Horton, *In Hope of Liberty,* 231.

[28]Still, *Underground Railroad,* 82-83; See also Arthur Cannon, *The Case of Passmore Williamson* (Philadelphia: Uriah Hunt & Son, 1856).

[29]Benjamin Quarles in Still, *Underground Railroad,* vi-vii.

[30]Horton, *In Hope of Liberty,* 141; William Douglass, *Annals of the First African Church in the United States of America* (Philadelphia: King and Baird, 1862), 94; and Richard Allen, *The Life Experience and Gospel Labor of the Right Reverend Richard Allen* (1887; reprint, New York: Abingdon Press, 1960

[31]Paul Russo, "Hinsonville, 1829-1868: A Sketch of a Chester County Afro-American Community," (unpublished manuscript, 1974). Lincoln University Archives.

[32]Interview with Hersey Gray, Oxford, PA: July 21, 2000; interview with Sarah Wesley, Oxford, PA: July 21, 2000.

[33]Gray interview.

[34]Pauli Murray, *Proud Shoes* (New York: Harper, 1956), 94-95. Murray is a descendant of the Fitzgerald family, free blacks who settled in Oxford in the 1850s. Her memoir is based on the reminiscences of aunts, uncles and grandparents.

[35]See *Oxford Press:* April 7, 1898; and Russo, "Hinsonville," 29.

[36]See Florence S. Miller, *A Legacy of Learning: The History of the West Chester Area Schools* (West Chester, PA, 1994), 61; and *Daily Local:* July 29, 1887.

[37]U.S. Department of State, *Sixth Census* (Washington D.C.: 1841), 24-27; Turner, *Negro in Pennsylvania,* 79-88; Nash, *Forging Freedom,* 212-14.

[38]Still, *Underground Railroad,* 223-34.

[39]*West Chester Daily Republican:* September 11, 1883; and *West Chester Daily Local:* August 30, 1883.

[40]*West Chester Daily Local:* February 10, 1842.

[41]Shadd is mentioned as an important station master in several accounts, including: Smedley, *History of the Underground Railroad in Chester County,* 33, 337; Futhey & Cope, *History of Chester County,* 426-27; Turner, *Negro in Pennsylvania,* 240.

[42]*Chester County Tax Lists,* 1836 , 1850; and *Chester County Septennial Census,* 1835, 1842, Chester County Historical Society.

[43]Jane Rhodes, *Mary Ann Shadd Cary. The Black Press and Protest in the Nineteenth Century.* (Bloomington, IN: Indiana University Press, 1998), 14.

[44]"Minutes of the State Convention of the Coloured Citizens of Pennsylvania, convened at Harrisburg, December 13-14, 1848," in Philip S. Foner and George S. Walker, eds., *Proceedings of the Black State Conventions, 1840-1865* (Philadelphia: Temple University Press, 1979), 119-35; and Rhodes, *Mary Ann Shadd Cary,* 16- 20.

[45]Rhodes, *Mary Ann Shadd Cary,* 17-21.

[46]Mary Ann Shadd Cary quoted in *North Star:* March 23, 1849.

[47]Among blacks there existed caste system based on skin color. Those with lighter skin commanded a higher position in society, though "whiteness" was denied to anyone with African blood. Accordingly, United States Census takers were extremely careful in distinguishing "blacks" (defined as those having three-fourths or more of African blood) from "mulattoes" (three-eighths to five-eighths black blood), "quadroons" (one-fourth black blood) and "octoroons" (one-eighth or any trace of black blood." [See United States Department of State, *Sixth Census* (Washington D.C., 1841)]. Conversely, those blacks of biracial ancestry reversed the definitions to justify their social status. An octoroon had seven-eighths or more white blood, a quadroon three-fourths white blood, and a mulatto five-eighths to three-eighths white blood. Thus, an octoroon believed himself to be superior to a quadroon; a quadroon felt superior to a mulatto; and a mulatto felt superior to all who were less than mulattoes, though all mixed bloods were called "Mulattoes." [For more comprehensive treatments of the caste system among antebellum blacks, see: Ira Berlin, "The Structure of the Free Negro Caste in the Antebellum United States," *Journal of Social History* 9 (Spring 1976): 305-311; Willard B. Gatewood, *Aristocrats of Color: The Black Elite, 1880-1920* (Bloomington, IN: Indiana University Press, 1990), 7-29; and James Oliver Horton, *Free People of Color,* 122-44].

[48]Rhodes, *Mary Ann Shadd Cary,* 5.

[49]*West Chester Daily Local:* March 3, 1890.

[50]J. Smith Futhey and Gilbert Cope, *History of Chester County* (Philadelphia: Lippincott & Co., 1881); and Margaret L. Wolf, *A History of West Whiteland* (Exton, PA: West Whiteland Historical Commission, 1982), 18-19.

[51]*Jeffersonian:* November 7, 1868.

[52]*Oxford Press:* April 7, 1898.

[53]Account of Ann Price in *Daily Local:* July 8, 1901.

[54]David Evans, *Journal,* 213, 217.

[55]*Village Record:* August 9, 1850.

[56]Sara L. Oberholtzer, "Reminiscences of the Underground Railroad in Chester County." Cope Collection. CCHS.

[57]Arthur E. James, *The Potters and Potteries of Chester County, PA* (West Chester, PA: D. Edwards Biehn, 1945), 9.

[58]Smedley, *History of the Underground Railroad in Chester County,* 148.

[59]Ella Peart (daughter-in-law of Lewis Peart), "Recollections of the Underground Railroad," (April 1939), CCHS.

[60]Samuel W. Pennypacker, *Annals of Phoenixville and its Vicinity: From the Settlement to the Year 1871* (Philadelphia: Bavis & Pennypacker, 1872), 214; and *Friends Intelligencer:* October 5, 1895.

[61]David Evans, *Journal,* 215-18.

[62]Francis C. Taylor, *The Trackless Trail* (Kennett Square, PA, 1976), 26-28; and Walter Grayson, "Historical Sketch of the Underground Railroad," *Kennett Square Centennial Book* (Kennett, PA, 1955), 35.

[63]According to the 1850 Census for Chester County, the Quakers were not the largest religious denomination in the region. The Methodists operated 45 churches and had a total memebership of 15,825 congregants. The Quakers were the second largest, operating 37 meetings with a total membership of 14,475. They were followed by the Presbyterians (19 churches / 9,620 members), Baptists (21 churches / 6,770 members), Espicopalians (9 churches / 3,480 members), German Reformed (5 churches / 3,000 members), Lutheran (6 churches / 2,500 members), and Mennonite (4 churches / 1,200 members). The Quakers were, however, the wealthiest religious group, their church assets amounting to $67,200, compared to the Presbyterians' $58,800 and the Methodists' $46,050. All the other denominations

enjoyed significantly less financial support assets totaling $35,00 or less. [See *Seventh Census of the United States: 1850* (Washington D.C.: Robert Armstrong, 1853), 200-203].

[64]Thomas Garrett to William Lloyd Garrison: 12-5-1850 in McGowan, *Station Master,* 111-12.

[65]Thomas Garrett to William Still: n.d., 1854; 8-12-1856; 9-6-1857; 10-31-1857; 12-1-1860 in McGowan, *Station Master,* 97-99.

[66]Thomas Garrett to Sarah Bradford: 6 mo. - 1868 in McGowan, *Station Master,* 153-55.

[67]Thomas Slaughter, *Bloody Dawn: The Christiana Riot and Racial Violence in the Antebellum North* (New York: Oxford University Press, 1991); For a more Afrocentric treatment, see Ella Forbes, *But We Have No Country: The 1851 Christiana Resistance* (Cherry Hill, NJ: Africana Homestead Legacy Publishers, 1998).

[68]Frederick Douglass, *My Bondage and My Freedom* (1855) edited by Philip S. Foner. (New York: Dover Publications, 1969), 454-56.

[69]Russo, "Hinsonville," 40-43; and Murray, *Proud Shoes,* 95.

[70]Rhodes, *Mary Ann Shadd Cary,* 29-32.

[71]Mary Ann Shadd to Isaac Shadd, September 16, 1851 quoted in *ibid.,* 34.

[72]Rhodes, *Mary Ann Shadd Cary,* 47-134.

[73]David Evans, *Journal:* 12 month / 1 / 1850.

[74]Albert John Wahl sees this conflict as part of a much larger transition stage in American religion "from the old authoritarianism orthodoxy of the right to the post-Civil War religion of humanity on the far left." [See Wahl, "Progressive Friends," 320.] Nor was the Chester County schism unique. Indiana Yearly Meeting also experienced a similar conflict, nearly a decade earlier in 1842. Those more liberal Friends devoted to the cause of immediate emancipation were censured by the yearly meeting and, in 1843, formed their own Indiana Yearly Meeting of Anti-Slavery Friends. It was a much larger separation than what had occurred at Kennett, involving about 2,500 of the 25,000 Friends who belonged to Indiana Yearly Meeting. Like the Longwood Progressive Friends, however, the Indiana Anti-Slavery Friends were also marginalized by the larger Society of Friends. Both separations reflect the fact that there were, indeed, limits to Quaker abolitionism. 28. Wahl, "Progressive Friends," 65-83. [See Walter Edgerton, *A History of the Separation in Indiana Yearly Meeting of the Society of Friends in the Winter of 1842 and 1843 on the Anti-Slavery Question* (Cincinnati, 1856); Thomas Hamm, "Moral Choices: Two Indiana Quaker Communities and the Abolitionist Movement," *Indiana Magazine of History* (June 1991): 117-54; and Ryan Jordan, "The Indiana Separation of 1842 and the Limits of Quaker Anti-Slavery," *Quaker History* (Spring 2000): 1-27].

[75]Pennsylvania Yearly Meeting of Progressive Friends (hereafter "PYMPF"), *Proceedings* (1853), 5. For a more detailed account of the founding of this group see Wahl, "Progressive Friends," 54-83.

[76]*Ibid.,* 6.

[77]For a more thorough treatment of the reciprocal influence between abolitionism and women's rights, see: Julie Roy Jeffrey, *The Great Silent Army of Abolitionism: Ordinary Women in the Anti-Slavery Movement* (Chapel Hill: University of North Carolina, 1998); and Aileen S. Kraditor, *Means and Ends in American Abolitionism. Garrison and His Critics on Strategy and Tactics, 1834-1850.* (New York: Random House, 1967), Chapter 2.

[78]"Slavery," PYMPF, *Proceedings* (1856), 43-44.

[79]"Slavery," PYMPF, *Proceedings* (1857), 13-15.

[80]*Jeffersonian and Democratic Herald:* March 25, 1854.

[81]*Pennsylvania Freeman:* February 23, March 30 , May 4, 1854.

[82]"Caste," PYMPF, *Proceedings* (1858), 35.

[83]"Complexional Distinctions," PYMPF, *Proceedings* (1863), 16.

[84]*Ibid.;* and "Caste," PYMPF, *Proceedings* (1858), 35.

[85]Thomas Whitson quoted in *Pennsylvania Freeman:* November 4, 1853.

[86]Lucretia Mott to Martha Wright, 12-5-1861. Friends Historical Library.

[87]Still, *Underground Railroad,* 712; and Wahl, "Progressive Friends," 292.

President Lincoln's Emancipation Proclamation

Abraham Lincoln,
President of the United States,
by virtue of the power in me vested
as Commander in Chief of the Army and
Navy of the United States, in time of
actual armed rebellion against the authority
and government of the United States, and as a fit and necessary war measure for suppress
ing said rebellion, do on this first day of January, in the year of our … thousand
eight hundred and sixty three, and in accordance with my purpose so to do … ned for the
full period of one hundred days from the day of the first above mentioned orde… States
and parts of States wherein the people thereof respectively are this day in rebellion … the
following, to wit: Arkansas, Texas, Louisiana — except the parishes of … es,
Jefferson, St. John, St. Charles, St. James, Ascension, Assumption, Terre… ary,
St. Martin, and Orleans, including the city of New Orleans — Mississippi, … ia,
South Carolina, North Carolina, and Virginia — except the forty eight count… nia,
and also the counties of Berkeley, Accomac, Northampton, Elizabeth City, Yo… lk,
including the cities of Norfolk and Portsmouth, and which excepted parts … isely
as if this proclamation were not issued.
And by virtue of the power and for the purpose aforesaid, I do ord… all
persons held as slaves within said designated States and parts of Sta… forward
shall be free; and that the executive government of the United States, … ilitary
and naval authorities thereof will recognize and maintain the freedom of …
And I hereby enjoin upon the people so declared to be free to a…
unless in necessary self defense; and I recommend to them that in a…
labor faithfully for reasonable wages.
And I further declare and make known that …
be received into the armed service of the United States, to g…
places, and to man vessels of all sorts in said service.
And upon this, sincerely believed to be an …
upon military necessity, I invoke the considerate jud…
Almighty
Executed and published by F. T. Butler, 1863

Figure 80: Emancipation Proclamation. (Courtesy of Library of Congress)

6.

Breaking *the* Line

Figure 81: Abraham Lincoln in 1863. (Courtesy of Library of Congress)

The election of Abraham Lincoln to the presidency in 1860 provoked a chain of events that not only led to civil war, but also to realizing the mutual desire that Chester County's radical abolitionists, both black and white, had for emancipation. While Quakers generally supported the goals of the president, wanting to see an end to slavery, there was some debate among Friends about how far they should cooperate with the government in wartime. Some members, adhering to the Society's long-standing testimony on peace, were conscientious objectors, even refusing to hire a substitute or pay a $300 commutation fee as required by the federal government's Conscription Act. Others, though a minority, went off to war or supported the government by paying war taxes.[1] Among the most influential Quakers, however, were the Longwood Progressive Friends who played an important role in persuading Lincoln to wed emancipation to his original war aim of preserving the Union. African Americans, on the other hand, embraced the war effort wholeheartedly. Initially serving in the Union Army as laborers, they eagerly enlisted as soldiers after March 1863 as a means for demonstrating their desire for full U.S. citizenship. Like the Quakers, black dedication to the principle of abolitionism, inspired the president's actions during the war.

Lincoln's election to the presidency can be attributed to increasing anti-slavery agitation which divided the old Democratic-Whig Party system into sectional wings during the late 1850s. The initial battleground was Kansas where anti-slavery and pro-slavery forces established two, competing governments in the process of applying for statehood. The violence that broke out there in 1856 significantly weakened the influence of the Democrats in resolving the conflict. Subsequent events resulted in an irreparable split within the party.

The Dred Scott decision of 1857, for example, exacerbated tensions within the party by ruling that slavery could not be excluded from the territories, thereby repealing the Missouri Compromise. A year later, the Lincoln-Douglas debates, which would determine the Illinois senatorial campaign, forced Congressional Democrats to deal more proactively with the issue of slavery by stressing the immorality of the institution as well as Douglas' amoral approach to the problem. Finally, John Brown's failed attempt to instigate a slave insurrection at Harper's Ferry, Virginia, in 1859, provoked the widespread belief among southerners that all abolitionists were dangerous fanatics, bent on eliminating slavery at any cost.[2] By 1860, the Democrats were divided along anti-slavery and pro-slavery lines. Abolitionists, who had been marginalized in the old system, had formed an alliance with former Whigs and anti-slavery Democrats, creating a new, Republican Party.[3] Abraham Lincoln emerged as the party's most viable candidate for president.

Prior to 1860, Lincoln and his anti-slavery views were not widely known outside of his home state of Illinois. That he was able

Figure 82: **John Brown.** In 1859, radical abolitionist John Brown led a group of 16 whites and 5 blacks to seize a federal arsenal in Harpers Ferry, Virginia and led an armed insurrection against local slaveholders. Brown was captured after a bloody ordeal with federal troops led by a Colonel Robert E. Lee. At his trial, the radical's words inspired Northerners and scared Southerners and foretold the violence that was to come. (Chester County Historical Society)

to gain greater exposure in the East was due, in part, to a campaign biography that was published in Chester County. Lincoln's campaign manager, Jesse Fell, realized the need early on to introduce his candidate to the eastern political establishment and persuaded him to write a brief account of his life for that purpose. Fell, an attorney and native of New Garden Township, first suggested the idea in 1858 after touring the eastern states to gauge public opinion for a possible presidential campaign. "What the Republican Party wants, to ensure success in 1860, is a man of popular origin, of acknowledged ability, commitment against slavery aggressions, who has no record to defend, and no radicalism of an offensive character," he told Lincoln, who was running for the United States Senate at the time. "Your debates with Senator [Stephen] Douglas have demonstrated your ability, your devotion to freedom; you have no embarrassing record; you have sprung from the humble walks of life, sharing its toils and trials; and if we can only get these facts sufficiently before the people, there is some chance that you can be made a formidable, if not a successful, candidate for the presidency."[4]

Lincoln initially dismissed the suggestion, stating that there were other Republicans who were "much better known to the people" than himself and that there was "nothing in my early history that would interest you or anybody else."[5] But Fell persevered. The following year, 1859, he tested the political waters of Pennsylvania again. By that time, Lincoln's speeches from his previous senatorial campaign had been published in the East and his moderate position on the slavery question was much more appealing to electors than other Republican hopefuls such as Senator Simon Cameron of Pennsylvania, William Seward of New York, or Samuel Chase of Ohio. Lincoln still needed to reach the common man, though. He finally agreed to write a few pages about his life and, on December 20, 1859, he gave a short, humble account to Fell with the postscript: "There is not much of it, for the reason, I suppose, that there is not much of me."[6]

Fell made some additions relating to Lincoln's political history and quickly dispatched the account to Joseph J. Lewis, a Republican delegate from West Chester. Lewis rewrote and lengthened the piece into a 2,500-word essay, which was forwarded to Samuel R. Downing, editor of *The Chester County Times.* Lewis and Fell also made sure to

Figure 83, Catalog 76: **Lincoln Building.** at 28 West Market St., West Chester, where Lincoln's 1860 campaign biography was published by The Chester County Times.

distribute copies to influential editors throughout Pennsylvania and other states.[7] It was a political masterstroke. Not only did the biography familiarize eastern voters with the Illinois candidate, but alleviated any concerns they might have had about his position on slavery.

The biography gave greater exposure to Lincoln's shrewd insistence that the South had a constitutional right to preserve slavery while also demanding that Congress prohibit its extension.[8] Not only did the strategy unite the competing factions within the Republican Party, but convinced Pennsylvanians to abandon their native son, Simon Cameron, and rally for the Illinois Rail Splitter. Thus, in May, Lincoln was able to secure the Republican nomination for president on the third ballot at the party's national convention in Chicago. But he still faced a tough battle, even in Republican strongholds like Chester County.

The Jeffersonian, West Chester's Democrat-sponsored newspaper, spread sensationalist rhetoric, painting the specter of an integrated North if Lincoln won. Reporting that Lincoln "has left no room for doubt about his intention to put slavery in progress of ultimate extinction," the newspaper predicted that the "four million Negroes who are now slaves in the South," would, if Lincoln wins, "over-run Pennsylvania, not leaving an acre of our soil untrodden by their gizzard feet." These "poor, dependent Negroes would come among us," predicted *The Jeffersonian,* "and what food or clothing they could not get by begging they would take by stealth." Raising the strong possibility of white displacement in the labor force, the newspaper called on white "mechanics and workingmen to protect themselves from the degrading and injurious competition of free Negro labor by opposing the election of Abraham Lincoln."[9]

Because the Democrats were divided over slavery, however, the party split into sectional factions, paving the way for Lincoln's victory. Winning a clear majority of the electoral votes and 40% of the popular vote, Lincoln won the general election on November 13th. Of the 13,244 votes cast in Chester County, he secured 7,771 votes, polling highest in those townships with a significant Quaker population, like West Chester, the Nantmeals, Tredyffrin, and Kennett. Townships heavily populated by the Scotch-Irish and Germans and traditionally pro-slavery in sentiment—East Nottingham, Lower Oxford, the Pikelands, West Vincent and Sadsbury—voted for John C. Breckinridge, the Democrat candidate from Kentucky.[10] Now Chester County, like the nation itself, would wait to see if Lincoln would uphold the delicate balance he had

Figure 84, Catalog 75: STATUE OF ABRAHAM LINCOLN.

earlier articulated between respecting the constitutional rights of the South to retain their slaves and preventing the extension of the peculiar institution.

Throughout his political career, Lincoln often evoked the principles of the *Declaration of Independence* to remind himself of the obligation he had as a public servant.[11] "I have never had a feeling politically that did not spring from the sentiments embodied in the *Declaration,*" he insisted in 1861. "It is the great charter of freedom that enables the world to grow and to expand into the universal liberty of mankind."[12] Lincoln would find great strength in that principle during his presidency and vowed to enforce it from the very beginning.

On February 22, 1861, the president-elect, traveling from his home of Springfield, Illinois to Washington where he would assume executive office, made his first visit to Philadelphia. As he stood before Independence Hall, he admitted to being "filled with deep emotion" and spoke of his reverence for the *Declaration* which gave "liberty, not alone to the people of this country, but hope to the world for all future time." Addressing the impending crisis, Lincoln added: "If this country cannot be saved without giving up that principle—I would rather be assassinated on this spot than to surrender to it. It is the only principle that I am willing to live by, and, in the pleasure of Almighty God, die by."[13] It was because of his strong belief in the *Declaration* that Lincoln rejected the notion that the rights of liberty and the pursuit of happiness were confined to the white race.

Figure 85: Oliver Johnson, a member of Longwood Meeting, met with President Lincoln on June 20, 1862 to persuade him to free slaves. (From a carte-de-visite by Charles D. Fredericks and Co., New York, ca. 1863)

Lincoln had always been morally opposed to slavery, an institution "founded on a monstrous injustice." Slavery, he believed, "deprives our republican example of its just influence in the world and enables the enemies of free institutions—with plausibility—to taunt us as hypocrites because it forces so many really good men amongst ourselves into an open war with the very fundamental principles of the *Declaration of Independence,* insisting that there is no right principle of action, but *self-interest.*"[14]

Curiously, for as great an emphasis as Lincoln placed on the principle of liberty, he did nothing to abolish slavery when he became president. In fact, he believed that the president did not have the power to eliminate slavery, and assured southerners that he had no intention of interfering with the institution in their states. Later, when civil war broke out, he reassured the loyal border states of his promise and revoked orders by Union generals emancipating the slaves of Confederates in Missouri.[15] There were those, of course, who saw a the contradiction between his rhetoric and actions.

Lucretia Mott wrote that the abolitionists had "little faith in 'Old Abe' and his cabinet." They feared that he would make "mean compromises" with the South and that all his "political speeches are lacking in a feeling heart for the slave."[16] Pennsylvania's Quakers, in general, had grave reservations about securing emancipation through military means because of their long-standing testimony on peace. But Progressive Friends were more sympathetic to Lincoln's position.

On June 20, 1862, Lincoln met with six members of the Longwood Progressive Friends Meeting. Thomas Garrett, Oliver Johnson, William Barnard, Eliza Agnew,

Dinah Mendenhall and Alice Hambleton were ushered into president's office, where they were received with "something more than official courtesy." Having descended from Quakers himself, Lincoln was comfortable with Friends. He understood and appreciated their firm reliance on an Inner Light, as well the circumstances leading to the establishment of the Progressive Friends Meeting.[17] Furthermore, the Progressives had already endeared themselves to Lincoln by sympathizing with his position.

Unlike Philadelphia Yearly Meeting, which condemned the war, the Progressives understood Lincoln's constitutional responsibility to preserve the Union by forcible means. "We have no hesitancy," they said, "in declaring that the government—measuring it by its constitutional obligations—had no alternative but to seek to suppress this treasonable outbreak by all means and forces at its disposal, or else to betray the sacred trusts committed to it by the people; and therefore, throughout this fearful struggle, it has our sympathy, and desire for its success."[18] However, the delegation did implore Lincoln to emancipate the slaves.

Insisting that their "clients are 4 million slaves who cannot speak for themselves," Oliver Johnson presented the president with the memorial.[19] Then, William Barnard expressed the group's "earnest desire" that the president, "under divine guidance, be led to free the slaves," and thus "save the nation from destruction." Not only would such an action enable him to secure a favorable place in history, but to "secure the blessing of God."[20]

Lincoln's response revealed the complexity of the situation he faced. While he agreed that slavery was wrong, he questioned the method of its removal. The primary difficulty, he said, was *enforcement.* So far as he could see, a decree "could not be enforced in that part of the country now. Would a proclamation of freedom be anymore effective?" He honestly didn't know. At the same time Lincoln admitted that he was "deeply sensible of his need for Divine assistance" and that he "sometimes thought that perhaps he might be an instrument in God's hand of accomplishing some great work and that he certainly was not unwilling to be." He suggested, however, that God's way of achieving emancipation may be different from theirs. Nevertheless, Lincoln insisted that it would be his "earnest endeavor, with a firm reliance upon the Divine arm, and seeking light from above, to do his duty in the place to which he had been called."[21]

Just over a month later, however, Lincoln insisted that his primary goal was to save the Union, with or without slavery: "If I could save the Union without freeing any slave, I would do it; and if I could save it by freeing all the slaves, I would do it; and if I could do it by freeing some and leaving others alone, I would also do that," he wrote Horace Greeley, the influential abolitionist editor of *The New York Tribune,* who printed the response in August 1862. "What I do about slavery and the colored race," he concluded, I do because I believe it helps to save the Union."[22]

Lincoln had no choice but to proceed cautiously on the issue of slavery. While he had a strong moral revulsion against the institution, the idea of emancipating slaves by executive order went against his political instincts. He realized that he had been elected on an anti-slavery platform and he knew that as president, he had sworn to uphold the Constitution, which placed strict limits on his ability to interfere with slavery. What's more, Lincoln realized that a president who defied public opinion could lose his capacity to lead altogether and that most northern whites viewed black people as inferior. Many also believed that emancipation would trigger a massive influx of former slaves into the North, where they would compete for white men's jobs. Race riots in New York, Philadelphia, and Buffalo dramatized these white attitudes. Under these circumstances, if Lincoln moved too quickly on emancipation, he risked offending the border states, and increased the Democrats' chances for political victory in 1864. Yet if he didn't make a move, Lincoln would alienate abolitionists and lose the support of Radical Republicans which he simply could not afford to do.[23] As the casualty lists grew to appalling proportions, however, he began to reconsider the meaning of the war in a way that went far beyond politics and public opinion.

Lincoln began to question why the South was winning the war if, in fact, the will of God prevails. "God wills this contest, and wills that it should not end,' he wrote in September 1862 in a personal reflection known as his "Meditation on the Divine Will." "By His mere quiet power, He could have either saved or destroyed the Union without human contest." Lincoln was now convinced that he was "an instrument in God's hands for accomplishing a great work" and he looked for some kind of sign to provide him with direction.[24] That sign arrived on September 17, 1862, with the Union victory at Antietam. Five days later, Lincoln, despite the divided opinion of his own cabinet, issued the *Emancipation Proclamation,* declaring that unless the rebellious states returned to the Union by January 1, 1863, he would declare their slaves "forever free." When the Confederacy rejected his demand to free their slaves, Lincoln, on New Year's Day, 1863, issued the *Proclamation* as he had promised, calling it an "act of justice warranted by the Constitution upon military necessity."[26]

The Progressive Friends were not satisfied with the proclamation. Thomas Garrett complained to William Lloyd Garrison that Lincoln's refusal to free the slaves in the border states "will lead to more difficulty both with master and slave." "I believe that it would have been better," he continued, "for the whole country if a general proclamation of emancipation had been declared by the president, to take effect at once, paying reasonable compensation to all loyal slave holders in the border states, as a matter of expediency. Had such a proclamation been made, it would have done more toward stopping the effusion of blood than any other plan that would be adopted, and, in the end, cost the government less."[27] Predictably, the Progressives continued to send their petitions to Congress calling for the extension of Lincoln's proclamation to the border states as well.[28]

While the *Emancipation Proclamation* had no immediate impact on slavery, affecting only those slaves living in the unconquered portion of the Confederacy, it did represent a sea change in Lincoln's view of the war. What had begun as a war to save the Union now also became a struggle that, if victorious, would free the slaves. It also liberated Lincoln from the sharp tension he once felt between those two objectives, and reflected

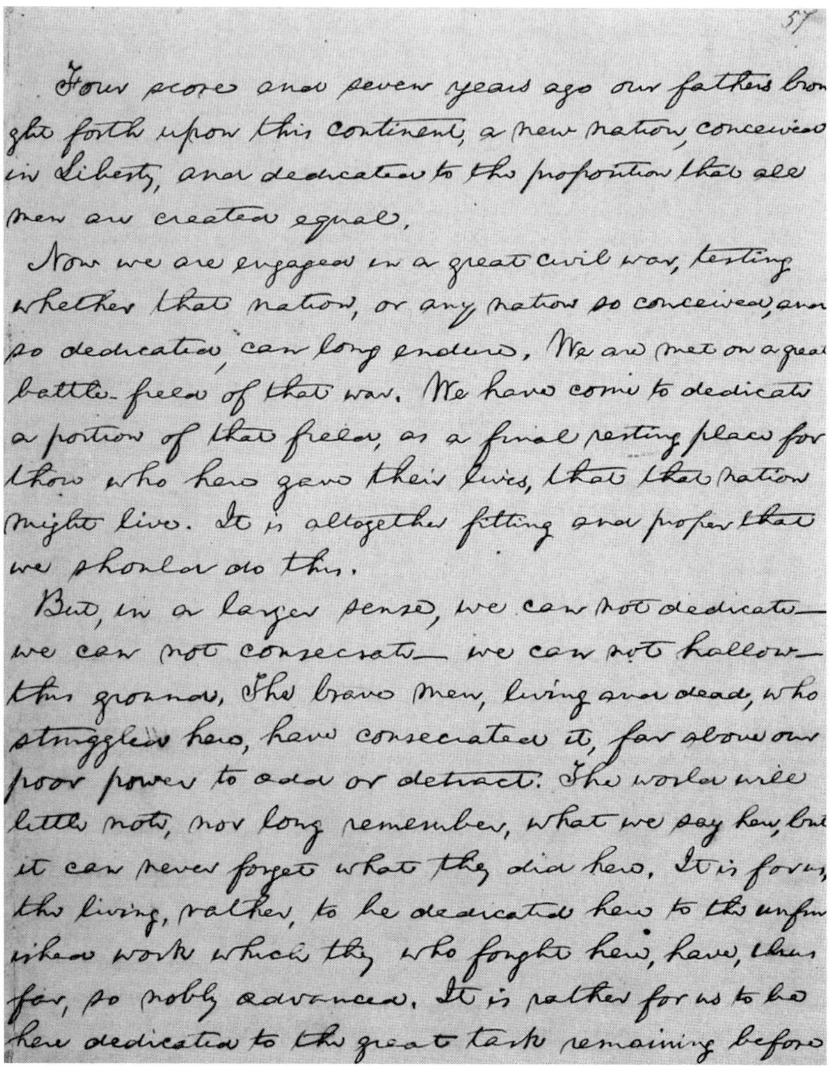
57

Four score and seven years ago our fathers brought forth upon this continent, a new nation, conceived in Liberty, and dedicated to the proposition that all men are created equal,

Now we are engaged in a great civil war, testing whether that nation, or any nation so conceived, and so dedicated, can long endure, We are met on a great battle-field of that war. We have come to dedicate a portion of that field, as a final resting place for those who here gave their lives, that that nation might live. It is altogether fitting and proper that we should do this.

But, in a larger sense, we can not dedicate— we can not consecrate— we can not hallow— this ground, The brave men, living and dead, who struggled here, have consecrated it, far above our poor power to add or detract. The world will little note, nor long remember, what we say here, but it can never forget what they did here, It is for us, the living, rather, to be dedicated here to the unfinished work which they who fought here, have, thus far, so nobly advanced. It is rather for us to be here dedicated to the great task remaining before

Figure 86: The Gettysburg Address, delivered by President Abraham Lincoln on November 19, 1863, redefined the meaning of the Civil War as a struggle not only to preserve the Union, but to emancipate all the slaves. (Courtesy of Library of Congress)

Figure 87, Catalog 81: UNIDENTIFIED BLACK UNION SOLDIER FROM CHESTER COUNTY.

his new-found realization that he could not save the Union "half free and half slave" as he had previously asserted. On November 19, 1863, Lincoln articulated the clearest expression of these two, inextricable aims in his *Gettysburg Address.*

Only ten sentences, or 272 words in length, the *Gettysburg Address* appealed to the reverence Americans held for the *Declaration of Independence* and redefined the meaning of that document for future generations. He called on his countrymen to rededicate themselves to the principle "that all men are created equal" so that "this nation, under God, shall have a new birth of freedom." It was a masterful stroke of oratory, insisting that the American people must, in consistency with the principles of that *Declaration,* relinquish their prejudice against the black man. Those two sentiments could no longer coexist if the great sacrifice of "those who here gave their lives that this nation might live" was to be duly honored.[29] By linking the sacrifice of the Union soldiers at Gettysburg to the principles of the *Declaration of Independence,* the president appealed to the American people's fundamental sense of justice and morality and gave a powerful new meaning to the proposition that "all men were created equal."[30]

The *Emancipation Proclamation* also forced Lincoln to reconsider the role black troops might play in the outcome of the war. Strong opposition in the North, as well as a lingering prejudice that blacks were intellectually and socially inferior, limited most black involvement to driving supply wagons, burying the dead after battle, and building railroads for the war effort. Pressured by a series of Union defeats in 1862 and a drop in white enlistments, Congress repealed a 1792 ordinance barring "persons of color" from serving in the militia and passed a Confiscation Act which empowered the president to "use as many persons of African descent" as he needed "for suppression of the Rebellion." The South Carolina Sea Islands, which had come under Union control by August 1862, was the first to act on the new legislation, organizing two black regiments.[31] Still, Lincoln refused to raise a large black army on political grounds. "To arm the Negroes," he told his abolitionist critics, "would turn 50,000 bayonets from the loyal Border States against us that were for us."[32]

Black leaders continued to urge the necessity of enlisting black troops, realizing that if the black man proved his patriotism and courage on the battlefield, the nation would be morally obligated to grant him first-class citizenship. No one expressed those sentiments more eloquently than Frederick Douglass. Attacking the inconsistency of Lincoln's position of making repeated calls for men only to let "Indo-Caucasian hands" fight, the famous black orator insisted that "once the black man gets upon his person the brass letters 'U.S.', a musket on his shoulder, and bullets in his pocket, there is no power on earth that can deny that he has earned the right to citizenship in the United States."[33] The debate continued until January 1, 1863 when the *Emancipation Proclamation* was made official. Having freed, by executive order, those slaves in the South, Lincoln could no longer deny the black man the opportunity to fight. When some Union generals complained about the president's change of heart, Lincoln was swift in his response. "You say you will not fight to free Negroes," he shot back. "Some of them seem to be willing to fight for you. When victory is won, there will be some black men who can remember that, with silent tongue and clenched teeth, and steady eye and well-poised bayonet, they have helped mankind on to this great consummation. I fear, however, that there will also be some white ones, unable to forget that with malignant heart and deceitful speech, they strove to hinder it."[34]

When the Proclamation went into effect on New Year's Day, Chester County's free black community celebrated. West Chester's blacks hung flags from their windows in the morning, and a big rally was held in the afternoon at the Ashmun Institute, a institution of higher education for blacks, in Lower Oxford.[35] They knew it was only a matter time before they, too, would be allowed to fight.

On February 13, 1863, Senator Charles Sumner of Massachusetts presented a bill in Congress proposing the "enlistment of 300,000 colored troops." Although the bill was defeated, the state's governor John A. Andrew requested and received authorization from Secretary of War Edwin M. Stanton to organize a colored regiment of volunteers to serve for three years. In Massachusetts only 100 men volunteered during the first six weeks of recruitment. The state's black men were insulted by the fact that the regiment would be headed by only white officers and by the fact that black soldiers would receive lower pay than white soldiers. Disillusioned by the turnout, Andrew organized a committee of prominent citizens and black leaders to supervise the recruitment of black troops. Within two month's time, the committee collected $5,000 and established a line of recruiting posts from Boston to St. Louis. Soon the quota was raised, and 1,000 freedmen and former slaves from throughout the Union became part of the "54th Regiment

Figure 88: U.S. Colored Troops. (Courtesy Library of Congress)

Massachusetts Volunteer Infantry, Colored."[36]

"A large number of colored men in Chester County are wanting to organize into companies for the war," reported West Chester's *Village Record* on June 13, 1863. "As yet there is no authority to enlist them in this state, as far as we can learn. Some of them are preparing to go to Massachusetts where they will be received."[37] Among their numbers were: Solomon Anderson, Samuel Berry, Lemuel Blake, George Brown, Jesse H. Brown, Morris Brown, Andrew Clark, Thomas F. Cooper, George Counsel, John W. Dixon, Solomon Hazard, Lewis Hercules, Clayton Johnson, , William Jones, George F. Merriman, Jeremiah Parker, Charles Henry Preston, William Rigby, John Shirley, Edward H. Smith, Enos Spriggs, George R. Vanleer, Stephen Washington, William H. Washington, and Samuel R. Wilson, all of West Chester; James Cole, George, Wesley and William Jay, and Albert Walls, all of Oxford; Josiah Cole, John Henson, Joseph Jones, William F. Pennington, and John Smith, all of Coatesville; and John Douglass, George Farmer, Abraham and London Glasgow of Unionville.[38] Most were farmers in their mid-to-late twenties, who were mustered into Company B. Five demonstrated leadership abilities that earned them the rank of a non-commissioned officer, including: Solomon Anderson; George Farmer; Abraham Glasgow; George F. Merriman; and William Rigby. [See Appendix C: Chester Countians in the Massachusetts 54th Colored Regiment]

Commanded by Colonel Robert Gould Shaw, the twenty-five-year-old scion of a wealthy and socially prominent Boston abolitionist family, all of these men understood the severe consequences of enlisting. Shortly after the 54th was mustered into service, the Confederate Congress passed an act stating its intention to "put to death," if captured, "any Negro" as well as "white commissioned officer [who] shall command, prepare or aid Negroes in arms against the Confederate States."[39]

In Chester County, as in most of the North, there were mixed feelings about blacks and whites fighting in the same army. Thomas Garrett, who had long advocated peaceful abolitionism, confessed that he fell short of living up to those principles when it came to black recruitment. In an 1864 letter to William Still, he wrote that he was sending the Philadelphia agent a young runaway slave who "desires to join the army and fight for the North." Garrett requests that Still inform him when the fugitive is "snugly fixed in his regimentals, so that I may send word to his wife." In a postscript to the letter, Garrett wonders: "Am I not naughty, being a professed non-resistant to advise this poor fellow to serve Father Abraham [Lincoln]?"[40]

Greater concern over arming black soldiers and racial equality was voiced among the men of the 97th Pennsylvania, composed primarily of men from Chester and Delaware counties. "There is a Nigger Regiment at Port Royal under General Hunter," wrote Robert Lewis of the 97th. "The other day one of our corporals was at their camp and a sambo soldier came up and said, 'Are you a corporal?' 'Yes,' answered the 97th. 'I am too,' said the nigger. 'What do you think of the war now?'"[41] Samuel Day, a twenty-two-year-old private of the 97th, complained that black troops were "creating hard feelings among the soldiers of this division." Among his charges were that the blacks enjoyed "better uniforms" than the white troops, and a "choice piece of ground to encamp upon." "The nigger slaves is far better off than thousands of white soldiers, and I would not think the government would of suffered this to be so," he concluded.[42] There were others, however, who resigned themselves to the new reality of fighting alongside black troops.

"I'm not an abolitionist in the common acceptance of the word," insisted Nathan Pennypacker of the Exton Guards. "But I think the Rebels have forfeited all claims upon our government and slavery should be sacrificed for UNION."[43] Similarly, a notice in the *Village Record* of July 7, 1863, read: "We understand that about sixty colored men have left West Chester and gone in the U.S. service as soldiers. This will save that number of white men from being drafted. Who objects to this?"[44] Levi Crowl of Oxford, a lieutenant in the 124th Pennsylvania, put it most succinctly, "the nigger might as well fight as the white man."[45]

White skepticism towards black Union soldiers would change after the 54th's valiant assault at Fort Wagner on July 18, 1863. The 54th spearheaded a three-pronged attack aimed at capturing the necklace of heavily fortified islands that dotted the harbor of Charleston, S.C. If Wagner could be taken, the Federals could launch a major assault further south on Fort Sumter, which controlled access to the harbor. From there, it would only be a matter of time before Charleston fell.[46] By the end of the assault, the Union had lost 1,515 killed, wounded or missing. Of that number, 256 were black soldiers from the 54th Massachusetts, and 6 of those were from Chester County.[47]

From a military standpoint, Wagner was a costly failure. But the assault proved to be a turning point for blacks, serving to lessen lingering skepticism among whites about the combat readiness of African Americans. William H. Price, a white Chester County sailor whose ship bombarded Ft. Wagner from the sea coast, expressed his admiration for the 54th with the rhetorical question: "They then want to ask, 'will the nigger fight or not?'" Responding affirmatively, Price wrote, "a regiment of them went out a thousand strong, charged upon the mouth of the cannon, and only three hundred of them came out. Do you call that fighting or not?"[48]

The 54th's valiant example also opened the ranks of the Union Army to more than 180,000 African Americans who would infuse a new spirit into the war-weary North. Between June 17, 1863 and July 19, 1865, Camp William Penn outside of Philadelphia, the first and largest training facility of United States Colored Troops, trained nearly 16,000 soldiers for eleven regiments and one independent company. Many Chester Countians were among the 60 black regiments that saw combat during the war.[49] [See Appendix D: Chester Countians in the U.S. Colored Troops]

Time and again, black troops proved themselves every bit as effective on the battlefield as their white counterparts. Several Chester Countians from the 54th were wounded at Olustee during the Florida campaign of 1864, including Jeremiah Parker of West Chester and George Brown of Doe Run. Thomas Cooper, a twenty-one-year-old bricklayer from West Chester was mortally wounded in the same battle.[50] Others demonstrated exceptional leadership abilities, earning for themselves the rank of corporal, the highest that a black man could hold in the army at the time. Both George Farmer and Albert Glasgow of Unionville were promoted to corporal for their distinguished service in the 54th. Glasgow's efforts were especially impressive, having been wounded twice in South Carolina in 1863 and again at Olustee less than a year later. Tillman Valentine, an energetic farmhand from Pennsbury was made a non-commis-

Figure 89, Catalog 82: Christian Fleetwood, a graduate of the Ashmun Institute, was awarded the Congressional Medal of Honor on September 29, 1864 for his exemplary courage in battle.

sioned officer of his regiment, the 3rd United States Colored Troop.[51] And Christian Fleetwood, a graduate of the Ashmun Institute in Lower Oxford, was awarded the Congressional Medal of Honor on September 29, 1864 at the Battle of Chapin's Farm in Virginia. Although he was strongly recommended for a commission as second lieutenant, the military refused to make the exception.[52]

By the end of the Civil War, 186,000 blacks had served in the Union army, 500 or more from Chester County alone. Of the total number, 134,111 had escaped from slave states.[53] Fighting side by side with white soldiers helped African Americans overcome some of the prejudice that existed in the Union Army. According to Benjamin W. Jones, a Chester Countian who fought in a black regiment in the Florida campaign, significant strides were made between black and white soldiers as they marched into battle together. "We swept through the state like a band of brothers," he insisted, most likely exaggerating the reality. "There was no respecters of persons or colors. The nonproscriptive feeling has grown stronger and stronger. We marched together, eat and drink together, slept together and best of all *fight together like men* and *die together like soldiers* and lovers of the Union."[54]

Figure 90, Catalog 85: **Moses Hepburn, Jr.** proprietor of West Chester's Magnolia House Hotel, became one of the county's most successful black entrepreneurs at the turn of the nineteenth century.

Despite his enthusiasm for the improved state of race relations on the battlefield, Jones had to admit that little had changed on the home-front. "We have served the country for more than a year, deprived of full pay and a soldier's rights," he wrote in August 1864. All we have received from this Union is one encouragement—it acknowledges our bravery and our ability to fight. But this will not save our families from starvation or from the poor-house."[55] He would prove to be correct.

With the end of the Civil War in 1865 and the subsequent passage of the 13th Amendment abolishing slavery in the United States, Thomas Garrett and other Underground Railroad agents could rejoice that "the colored people by law, now have equal privileges with the white man." But they also realized that "much need[ed] to be done before they can fully enjoy the rights of United States citizenship."[56] Many former station masters turned their attention to the plight of the newly emancipated slaves in the southern states by joining the Freedmen's Association, which raised money and collected food and clothing for freed slaves who were living in abject poverty in areas captured by northern armies. Along with meeting these basic needs, they turned their attention to education. Having been prohibited from learning to read and write during their enslavement, freedmen were eager for schools and the former abolitionists organized simple classrooms for their instruction as rapidly as teachers could be found, until the early 1870s, when many of the Quaker agents turned their attentions closer to home.[57]

Among the many beneficiaries of Quaker philanthropy were Samuel and Leah Ruth, former slaves from South Carolina. With the aid of the Friends' Freedmen Association they settled in Ercildoun and began a threshing business. Samuel also learned to read and write, and, again with the help of Quakers, was reunited with his mother.[58] Similarly, Samuel and Elizabeth Davis were Virginia slaves whose freedom was bought by a Quaker family. Relocating in West Chester after the Civil War, the Davises were among the very few blacks who continued to attend the local Friends meeting. Elizabeth worked as a domestic in the home of Congressman Thomas S. Butler, a prominent Quaker, and their daughter, Julia, attended the borough's Quaker schools.[59] Solomon Asberry's circumstances were more unique.

Born into slavery, Asberry, a mulatto,

ran away from his Maryland master at the age of 15. He fled to Chester County where he attended Ashmun Institute, married and, later, joined the U.S. Colored troops. After the war, he settled in London Grove where he joined the Society of Friends. Both of his children were educated by Friends and they continued to worship among Quakers until the family moved to Downingtown sometime in the 1870s.[60]

Friends' acceptance of the Davis and Asberry families is most likely due to their exceptionally fair-skinned complexion, which made them almost indistinguishable from whites. In fact, Quakers, during the post-war era, continued to accept segregation as a necessary part of life. They lacked an appreciation for African-American culture, and tried to make the blacks they served through their philanthropic programs as much like whites as possible. In doing so, they were no better or worse than any other middle-class white denomination of the time period. Under these circumstances, blacks were forced to rely on each other in order to assimilate into mainstream society.

Ashmun Institute, which was renamed "Lincoln University" in honor of the assassinated president, was one of the leading institutions for black self-assertion, nationally as well as in Chester County. Rejecting the manual training instruction emphasized by Booker T. Washington's Tuskeegee Institute in Alabama, Lincoln offered an academic curriculum and expanded it's seminary to include a preparatory school, a college, business, law and medical training.[61]

African Americans also established new mutual aid societies, such as the Grand United Order of Tents, a West Chester society of "colored females for benevolent, charitable, beneficial, and protective purposes to its members."[62] Originally founded in 1847 to help runaway slaves find freedom in the North, the Order of Tents concentrated on providing blacks with education and health care after Emancipation. The organization was divided into districts, comprised of subordinate tents, such as the "Star of West Tent" chartered in 1865 and the "Lydia Tent," organized in 1905. Throughout the nineteenth and twentieth centuries, fraternal organizations like these assumed greater political importance as they mobilized against black voter discrimination and offered scholarship money to promising young African-American students.[63]

With the assistance of mutual aid societies, blacks began to take an active role in the commercial activity of Chester County. Limited by either law or custom and often by inadequate opportunities for training, some entered the restaurant, hotel and catering business, one of the few available opportunities open to blacks. Moses G. Hepburn, Jr., Charles H. Burns and James Spence, all established businesses in West Chester following the Civil War and sustained their commercial success well into the twentieth century. These black entrepreneurs soon became active in the civic life of West Chester, as the African-American community looked to them for leadership.[64]

Despite these isolated successes, Chester County's blacks generally found it difficult to integrate into white society. As the Reconstruction era yielded to Jim Crow, they discovered that the inter-racial cooperation inspired by the Underground Railroad had its limits. Sadly, the result was a divided legacy of race relations.

Endnotes *to* Chapter Six

[1]See Edwin B. Bronner, "A Time of Change: Philadelphia Yearly Meeting, 1861-1914," in *Friends in the Delaware Valley: Philadelphia Yearly Meeting, 1681-1981,* edited by John M. Moore. (Haverford, PA: Friends Historical Association, 1981), 112-16; Peter Brock, "The Quakers in the Civil War," *Pioneers of the Peaceable Kingdom* (Princeton: Princeton University, 1970); and Edward N. Wright, *Conscientious Objectors in the Civil War* (New York, 1961). It is interesting to note that neither the Hicksite or Orthodox Yearly Meetings made any reference to the Civil War in 1861 or 1862. While many Friends did come under disciplinary action during the war for supporting the conflict in one way or another and there were some disownments in each yearly meeting, the discipline was not nearly as severe as it had been during the American Revolution.

[2]It is interesting to note, that while contemporary accounts attribute the failure of John Brown's raid to the refusal of local slaves to join Brown's insurrection, at least one of the five blacks present at Harper's Ferry disputes those reports. Osborne Perry Anderson of West Fallowfield Township, Chester County, insists that "colored people, as a body, were well represented by numbers, both in the fight and in the number who suffered martyrdom afterward." Anderson, who met Brown at the Chatham, Ontario Anti-Slavery Convention in April 1858, was impressed by the radical abolitionist's admonition to accept the "Christian duty of every man" and "strike down slavery through the use of arms." Believing Brown to be "chosen by God to his great work," Anderson agreed to join in the insurrection.

On the morning of the raid, Anderson went out into the Virginia countryside and informed slaves of the bands plans to free them by insurrection. "Joy and hilarity beamed from every countenance," he wrote, "when they learned of our purpose to effect their liberation." Considering that seventeen of the insurrectionists were killed and Anderson was the only black to escape, he concludes that the four blacks who did die at Harper's Ferry or were hanged at Charlestown afterwards constituted "a proper percentage of colored men to give up their lives." "That hundreds of slaves were ready and would have joined in the work, had Captain Brown's sympathies not been aroused in favor of the families of his prisoners," Anderson added, "a very different result would have been seen, there is no question." [See Osborne P. Anderson, *A Voice From Harper's Ferry* (Washington D.C.: J.D. Enos, 1878)].

[3]Tyler N. Anbinder, *Nativism and Slavery: The Northern Know Nothings and the Politics of the 1850s* (New York: Oxford University Press, 1992); William E. Gienapp, *The Origins of the Republican Party, 1852-1856* (New York: Oxford University Press); and Eric Foner, *Free Soil, Free Labor, Free Men: The Ideology of the Republican Party Before the Civil War* (New York: Oxford University Press, 1970).

[4]Jesse W. Fell, "Story of the Lincoln Biography," March 1872. Chester County Historical Society. It is interesting to note that Lincoln's family had roots in Pennsylvania. His great-great-grandfather, Mordecai Lincoln came to the Keystone state in 1720 and settled near French Creek in Chester County, where he was one of three partners in the operation of Coventry Forge. In 1728, he took up residence in Amity (now Exeter) Township in Berks County where he married and leased a thousand-acre farm, which he later purchased. Mordecai's eldest son, John, who was the president's great-grandfather, bought several tracts of land in Lancaster and Berks counties, but sold them all in 1765 and moved to the Shenandoah Valley of Virginia. John's son, Abraham, the president's grandfather, was born in Pennsylvania in 1744, but emigrated with his father to Virginia and later to Kentucky. [See "Lincolns in Chester County Related to 'Old Abe'," *Village Record* (West Chester, PA): June 5, 1860; and "Lincoln Forbears settled in Berks," *Philadelphia Public Ledger:* February 8, 1925.]

[5]Abraham Lincoln (hereafter "AL") quoted in Fell, "Story of Lincoln Biography."

[6]*Ibid.*

[7]See Fell, "Story of Lincoln Biography"; S.K. Stevens, "Pennsylvania's Influence on Lincoln's Election," *The Archive* (Downingtown, PA): February 10, 1947; and Jane N. Magee, "Jesse Fell's Role In History Uncovered By County Woman," *Intelligencer Journal* (Lancaster, PA): September 29, 1952.

[8]"AL," *Chester County Times* (West Chester, PA): February 11, 1860; See also: AL, "Reply to Stephen Douglas in 7th Debate at Alton, Illinois," October 15, 1858, *Abraham Lincoln: Speeches and Writings, 1859-65,* edited by Don E. Fehrenbacher. (2 vols., New York: Library of America, 1989), I: 790-814; and AL, "First Inaugural Address," March 4, 1861, Fehrenbacher, *Lincoln Speeches,* II: 215.

[9]*Jeffersonian* (West Chester, PA): November 3, 1860.

[10]"Chester County Voting Returns for Presidential Election of 1860," *Jeffersonian:* November 10, 1860.

[11]James M. McPherson, *Abraham Lincoln and the Second American Revolution* (New York: Oxford, 1990), 115, 126.

[12]AL quoted in *ibid,* 24, 129.

[13]AL, "Speech at Independence Hall, Philadelphia, February 22, 1861," Fehrenbacher, *Speeches of AL,* II: 213-14.

[14]AL "Address to Illinois Legislature, "March 3, 1837. Fehrenbacher, Speeches of AL, I: 18; and AL,

"Speech on Kansas-Nebraska Act at Peoria, Illinois," October 16, 1854, Fehrenbacher, Speeches, I: 315.

[15]McPherson, *Lincoln and Second American Revolution,* 127.

[16]Lucretia Mott to Martha Wright: 11 mo.-6-1861, Mott Manuscripts, Friends Historical Library, Swarthmore College.

[17]Lincoln stated on more than one occasion that his family "were originally Quakers, though in later times they have fallen away from the peculiar habits of that people." [See AL quoted by Henry Cadbury, "Lincoln's Quaker Ancestors," *Friends Journal* (February 15, 1962), 73.] For more information on Lincoln's Quaker background as well as his personal relations with Friends, See: Daniel Bassuk, *Abraham Lincoln and the Quakers* (Wallingford, PA: Pendle Hill, 1987); and D. Elton Trueblood, *Abraham Lincoln: Theologian of American Anguish* (New York: Harper & Row, 1973).

[18]Pennsylvania Yearly Meeting of Progressive Friends, "Memorial to President Lincoln," *Proceedings* (1862), 8, 17.

[19]Johnson quoted in *Village Record:* July 1, 1862.

[20]PYMPF, *Proceedings,* 1862, 11.

[21]AL quoted in *The New York Tribune:* June 21, 1862.

[22]AL, "Reply to Horace Greeley," August 22, 1862, Fehrenbacher, *Speeches of AL,* II: 357.

[23]John Hope Franklin, *The Emancipation Proclamation* (New York: Doubleday, 1963), 20.

[24]AL, "Meditation on the Divine Will," early September 1862, Fehrenbacher, *Speeches of AL,* II: 359.

[25]AL, "Preliminary Emancipation Proclamation," September 22, 1862, Fehrenbacher, *Speeches of AL,* II: 368-70.

[26]AL, "Final Emancipation Proclamation," January 1, 1863, Fehrenbacher, *Speeches of AL,* II: 425. Lerone Bennett, Jr., argues that Lincoln was a white supremacist who didn't care much for blacks and enjoyed the racist humor of the time. He makes a convincing case that the Emancipation Proclamation was a ploy designed to perpetuate slavery rather than extinguish it and that Lincoln would rather have sent black slaves back to Africa instead of integrating them into post-Civil War society. [See Bennett, *Forced into Glory: Abraham Lincoln's White Dream* (Chicago: Johnson Publishing Co., 2000)].

[27]Thomas Garrett to William L. Garrison: 1 mo.-5.1863, Boston Public Library.

[28]Progressive Friends, *Proceedings* (1863): 15.

[29]AL, "Gettysburg Address," November 19, 1863, Fehrenbacher, *Speeches of AL,* II: 536.

[30]Garry Wills, *Lincoln at Gettysburg. The Words That Remade America* (New York: Simon & Schuster, 1992), 33-34.

[31]James M. McPherson, *The Negro's Civil War. How American Blacks Felt and Acted During the War for the Union* (New York: Ballantine Books, 1991), 167.

[32]AL to Indiana Delegation, August 4, 1862, *Collected Works of Abraham Lincoln,* edited by Roy P. Basler. (9 vols., New Brunswick, NJ, 1955), V: 357.

[33]Frederick Douglass quoted in Geoffrey C. Ward, *The Civil War* (New York: Alfred A. Knopf, 1990), 247.

[34]AL quoted in Ward, *Civil War,* 247.

[35]Douglas R. Harper, *"If Thee Must Fight": A Civil War History of Chester County, Pennsylvania* (West Chester, PA: Chester County Historical Society, 1990), 285.

[36]Benjamin Quarles, *The Negro in the Civil War* (New York: Da Capo Press, 1989 paperback edition), 8-9.

[37]*Village Record:* June 13, 1863.

[38]Luis F. Emilio, *A Brave Black Regiment. History of the 54th Massachusetts Regiment* (1894) (Salem, NH: Ayer Company, 1990), appendix.

[39]Section IV of May 1, 1863 Act of the Congress of the Confederate States of America, quoted in *ibid.,* 7.

[40]Thomas Garrett to William Still: 1 mo.-23-1864, in Still, *Underground Railroad.*

[41]Robert Lewis to Lucilla Lewis, June 23, 1862. Chester County Historical Society.

[42]Samuel Day to ??, July 23, 1862. CCHS

[43]Nathan Pennypacker to Lide Pennypacker, January 11, 1863. CCHS.

[44]*Village Record* (West Chester, PA): July 7, 1863.

[45]Crowl quoted in Harper, *"If Thee Must Fight,"* 286.

[46]Peter M. Chaitin, *The Coastal War: Chesapeake Bay to Rio Grande.* (Alexandria, VA: Time-Life Books, 1984), 121-125.

[47]Ibid., 128; and Emilio, *A Brave Black Regiment,* 91.

[48]William H. Price quoted in *"If Thee Must Fight,"* 287-88.

[49]Frank H. Taylor, *Philadelphia in the Civil War, 1861-1865* (Philadelphia, 1913), 186-87.

[50]Harper, *"If Thee Must Fight,"* 288.

[51]*Ibid.*

[52]See Christian A. Fleetwood, *The Negro Soldier* (Washington D.C.: Howard University Press, 1894).

[53]Quarles, *Negro in the Civil War,* 20-21; and Harper, *"If Thee Must Fight,"* 287.

[54]Benjamin W. Jones quoted in *Village Record:* August 10, 1864.

[55]*Ibid.*

[56]Thomas Garrett to Aaron M. Powell: 4 mo.-5-1870, quoted in the *Liberator:* April 1870.

[57]Edwin B. Bronner, "A Time of Change: Philadelphia Yearly Meeting, 1861-1914, in *Friends in the Delaware Valley: Philadelphia Yearly Meeting, 1681-1981,* edited by John M. Moore. (Haverford, PA: Friends Historical Association, 1981), 116-118.

[58]Penny Washington, "Samuel Ruth and Maria Louisa Pinn-Ruth," (unpublished paper, 1998).

[59]Jervis Anderson, *Bayard Rustin: Troubles I've Seen* (New York: Harper Collins, 1997), 21-22. Julia Davis became a Quaker until she met and married Janifer Rustin of LaPlata, MD in 1891. Because he was a devout member of the AME Church, she converted to that faith to placate differences. They were the grandparents of civil rights leader, Bayard Rustin.

[60]Interview of Renee Carey, West Chester, PA: October 28, 2000.

[61]See "The Charter of Lincoln University, April 4, 1866," Lincoln University Archives; and Bond, *Education for Freedom,* 156-60.

[62]"Charter of the Independent Order Star of the West Tent, No. 6 of the Giddings and Jollifee Union," June 18, 1878.

[63]Charles H. Wesley, *The History of the National Association of Colored Womens' Clubs. A Legacy of Service* (Washington D.C., 1984).

[64]Robert Bussel, "The Most Indispensable Man in His Community: African American Entrepreneurs in West Chester, Pennsylvania, 1865-1925," *Pennsylvania History,* Vol. 65, No. 3 (Summer 1998): 324-49.

Epilogue

Figure 91: **Bayard Rustin** (Sketch by Dane Tilghman)

Figure 92, Catalog 103: **Bayard Rustin & Dr. Martin Luther King, Jr.** West Chester's Bayard Rustin (left) was a close aide to the Reverend Dr. Martin Luther King, Jr. during the Civil Rights movement of the 1960s, and organizer of the 1963 March on Washington.

Today, Chester County continues to celebrate the storied history of the Underground Railroad. But the divided sentiment that once existed over involvement in that clandestine movement has left the region with a mixed legacy of race relations.

During the four generations since the 13th and 14th Amendments guaranteed freedom and the rights of United States citizenship for African Americans, Chester County has been the scene of Jim Crow activity, fiercely-contested school desegregation struggles, and separate-but-equal public facilities. Freedom for black people was incomplete.

Racism came in many forms during the late nineteenth and twentieth centuries. One of the most shameful events occurred in August 1911, when Zack Walker, a black steel mill worker who had shot and killed a Coatesville policeman, was burned alive by a white mob in East Fallowfield. Had Walker been white, it has been argued, he would have been made to stand trial, been convicted and executed along the appropriate lines of justice. Instead, the actions of the mob were interpreted as racist. Not only did the incident capture national attention, but served as a catalyst for the NAACP's early campaign against lynching.[1]

The Ku Klux Klan, a secret organization dedicated to white supremacy, was never very large or popular in Chester County, but did stage cross burnings and drove away laborers and their families in the early twentieth century.[2]

School desegregation has also been slow in coming, particularly in the county seat of West Chester. While the townships had very small minority populations and were able to integrate their schools with little tension, West Chester struggled to desegregate its all-white elementary schools. Segregated schooling began in the borough in 1856. While West Chester's schools slowly desegrated during the twentieth century, it wasn't until 1977 that Schools Superintendent Dr. Donald E. Langlois implemented the first voluntary and comprehensive school desegregation program in the district. During the interim, blacks and whites were at odds with one another over a variety of issues, including inadequate facilities for black children, bussing into the borough, and the lack of black teachers to serve as role models for the children.[3]

Political change has also come slowly for West Chester's blacks. Only recently did the courts overturn an 1890 at-large election measure that prevented African Americans from successfully competing for council seats or voting a black mayor into office.

Even today, residential patterns throughout the county reflect the social and economic divide that persists in the region. Blacks and Hispanics tend to live in the low-income areas of the more populated boroughs, like West Chester, Kennett Square, Paoli, Coatesville, and Phoenixville, while the more affluent white population resides in suburban areas like Berwyn, Valley Forge, Chadds Ford and the Brandywine Valley. Thus, Chester County is not so much a

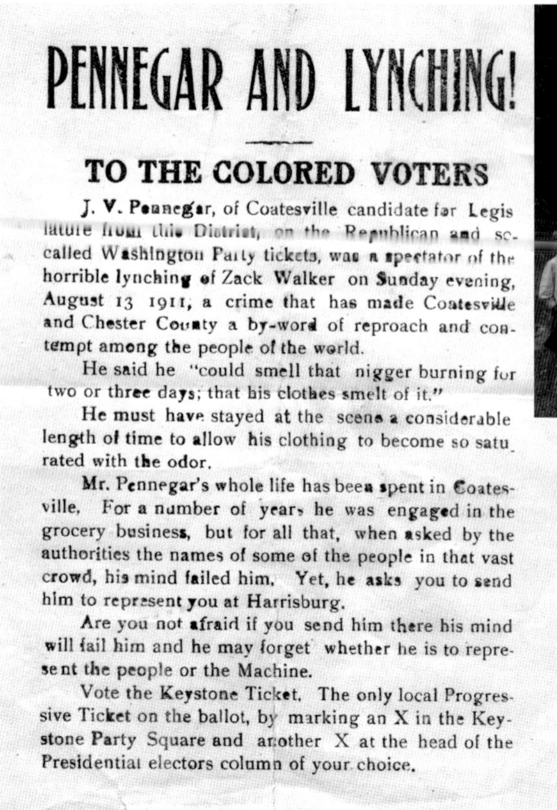

PENNEGAR AND LYNCHING!

TO THE COLORED VOTERS

J. V. Pennegar, of Coatesville candidate for Legislature from this District, on the Republican and so-called Washington Party tickets, was a spectator of the horrible lynching of Zack Walker on Sunday evening, August 13 1911, a crime that has made Coatesville and Chester County a by-word of reproach and contempt among the people of the world.

He said he "could smell that nigger burning for two or three days; that his clothes smelt of it."

He must have stayed at the scene a considerable length of time to allow his clothing to become so saturated with the odor.

Mr. Pennegar's whole life has been spent in Coatesville. For a number of years he was engaged in the grocery business, but for all that, when asked by the authorities the names of some of the people in that vast crowd, his mind failed him. Yet, he asks you to send him to represent you at Harrisburg.

Are you not afraid if you send him there his mind will fail him and he may forget whether he is to represent the people or the Machine.

Vote the Keystone Ticket. The only local Progressive Ticket on the ballot, by marking an X in the Keystone Party Square and another X at the head of the Presidential electors column of your choice.

Figure 93, Catalog 94: PENNEGAR FLIER. J.V. PENNEGAR WAS A COATESVILLE GROCER WHO RAN FOR THE STATE LEGISLATURE IN 1914 AS A REPUBLICAN. BEFORE THE ELECTION, HIS OPPOSITION POSTED FLIERS ABOUT HIS ALLEGED INVOLVEMENT IN THE WALKER LYNCHING, POINTING OUT THAT HE HAD BEEN AT THE LYNCHING LONG ENOUGH FOR HIS CLOTHES "TO SMELL LIKE BURNING FLESH FOR DAYS."

"patchwork quilt" as "independent communities" often divided along racial lines.

But there is still hope that both black and white people can learn some important lessons from this divided legacy as Chester County, like the nation, looks to the past to inform the current, national dialogue on race relations. The last decade of the twentieth century, in particular, has signaled hope that the interracial cooperation of the Underground Railroad that so many of us celebrate is still alive today.

In 1991, for example, when the Ku Klux Klan marched through the streets of downtown West Chester, the borough's black and white residents came together at a "Black and White Unity Day" that not only offset the Klan's rally, but solidified the community's commitment to interracial cooperation. Four years later, Henderson High School dedicated an historical marker to the late Bayard Rustin, a black alumnus who became a pivotal figure in the Civil Rights movement as an aide to Dr. Martin Luther King Jr. and chief organizer of the 1963 March on Washington. Though Rustin had, in the past, been a controversial figure because of his socialist political convictions as well as his homosexuality, the community was able to honor a native son for his important contribution to non-violence and civil rights.[4]

These are only two of many examples of interracial cooperation we can find if we look to Chester County's recent past. Perhaps they are not very consequential, but then, again, change begins with the individual and often happens when seemingly small actions and good will come together. "Racial equality," as Bayard Rustin once reminded us, "is a goal we must hold ever before us, for it not only confers dignity upon our struggle, but it should indicate to us how we must act toward one another today if we are to preserve for tomorrow the possibility of a just society."[5]

Endnotes *to* Epilogue

Figure 94, Catalog 92: ZACHARIAH WALKER LYNCHING. A SMALL CROWD GATHERED IN THE FIELD THE MORNING AFTER ZACHARIAH WALKER WAS LYNCHED BY A COATESVILLE MOB IN AUGUST OF 1911. THE LYNCHING, DEEMED A RACIALLY MOTIVATED INCIDENT, WAS THE CATALYST FOR THE NAACP'S CAMPAIGN TO SECURE THE PASSAGE OF AN ANTI-LYNCHING LAW.

[1]See Dennis B. Downey & Raymond Miltyser, *No Crooked Death. Coatesville, Pennsylvania and the Lynching of Zachariah Walker* (Chicago: University of Illinois Press, 1996); and William Ziglar, "Community of Trial: The Coatesville Lynching of 1911," *Pennsylvania Magazine of History and Biography,* Vol. CVI, No. 2 (April 1982): 245-70. Historians have attributed the Walker lynching to the displacement of long-time white residents of Coatesville by a massive influx of Eastern Europeans and southern blacks during the first decade of the 20th century, attracted by a booming steel industry. Coatesville's population had swelled from 5,500 residents to 11,000 in less than a decade. Walker himself had recently come North from Virginia to work at Worth's Steel Mill. The lynching was, according to historians, the "loosening of pent-up hostilities and a manifestation of social and labor conflict."

[2]Charles Hardy III, "The Ku Klux Klan in Pennsylvania" (unpublished paper delivered at the Philadelphia Academy of Fine Arts on July 17, 1997).

[3]Florence S. Miller, *A Legacy of Learning. The History of West Chester Area Schools* (West Chester, PA: West Chester Area School District, 1994), 61-80, 105-120, 183-191.

[4]*Daily Local News:* February 15, 1995.

[5]Bayard Rustin, "A Word to Black Students," *Bayard Rustin on the Black Experience in America* (New York: Bayard Rustin Fund, Incorporated, 1995)

Figure 95, Catalog 95: KU KLUX KLAN MARCH. ON JANUARY 12, 1991, THE PENNSYLVANIA KU KLUX KLAN MARCHED IN WEST CHESTER. IT TOOK THE MARCHERS TWELVE MINUTES TO COMPLETE THE SIX-BLOCK-LONG ROUTE. LOCAL POLICE OFFICERS AND STATE TROOPERS WERE ON HAND TO PREVENT A RIOT BETWEEN THE KKK AND COUNTER DEMONSTRATORS WHO LINED THE STREETS ALONG THE ROUTE.

Appendix A. Chester County Slaveholders *from the* 1780 Registry of Slaves

Name	Township	Number of Slaves Registered
Alexander, Patrick	Oxford	1
Allison, William	East Caln	3
Anderson, Patrick	Charlestown	1
Bell, John	West Fallowfield	8
Black, James	Westtown	1
Blair, Francis	Londonderry	2
Bodley, William	Charlestown	2
Bowen, John	Goshen	5
Bowen, Stephen	East Whitehead	1
Boyd, Andrew	Sadsbury	2
Boyd, Catharine	Sadsbury	1
Boyd, George	Unknown	1
Boyd, James	Londonderry	4
Boyd, Matthew	Sadsbury	1
Brittain, Richard	Tredyffrin	4
Brown, Elias	Charlestown	1
Bull, Thomas	East Nantmeal	2
Campbell, George	New London	1
Cheyney, Thomas, Esquire	Thornbury	2
Cloyd, John	Tredyffrin	2
Correy, Robert	New London	3
Cuthbert, John	East Nottingham	3
Darlington, Joseph	West Nantmeal	2
Davis, Benjamin	Tredyffrin	1
Davis, Dr. John	Tredyffrin	1
Davis, Llewellyn	Charlestown	1
Davis, Thomas	Sadsbury	1
Dewees, Colonel William	Tredyffrin	1
Dunwoody, James	West Whiteland	1

Name	Township	Number of Slaves Registered
Evans, Evan	London Britain	6
Evans, John	London Britain	9
Evans, John	Thornbury	1
Evans, Thomas	Thornbury	6
Finney, John	Londonderry	1
Foster, Reverend William	Sadsbury	3
Futhey, Samuel	West Fallowfield	3
Garrett, Mary	Goshen	3
Gibbs, Gilbert	West Caln	2
Gibson, Andrew	West Fallowfield	1
Gill, David	East Caln	1
Grace, Rebecca	Coventry	3
Graham, James	West Nantmeal	5
Graham, James	West Nantmeal	1
Griffith, Isaac	Willistown	1
Gronow, Lewis	Tredyffrin	5
Haines, Josiah	Goshen	1
Hanna, James	West Nantmeal	1
Hannum, James	West Marlborough	2
Havard, Ann	Tredyffrin	1
Havard, Sarah	Tredyffrin	2
Hayes, David	Oxford	2
Hayes, Margaret	Oxford	1
Henderson, James	East Nantmeal	1
Henderson, Matthew	East Nottingham	1
Hodgson, Abel	East Nottingham	3
Hood, Walter	Oxford	5
Humphrey, John	Charlestown	1
Hunter, Peter	West Nantmeal	2
Hutchinson, Joseph	Londonderry	1
Jacobs, John (Estate of)	West Whiteland	7
Johnson, Alexander	New London	1
Jones, Daniel	Londonderry	5
Kelso, Catherine	New London	1
Kelso, Mary	New London	1
Kennedy, Montgomery	Londonderry	2
Kennedy, Samuel (Heirs of)	Pikeland	3
Lloyd, David	East Whiteland	1
Luckie, Joseph	Oxford	1
Lunn, Thomas	London Britain	2
Mackey, John	New London	1
Maffett, Thomas	East Nottingham	3

Name	Township	Number of Slaves Registered
Mather, Peter	East Whiteland	1
May, Thomas	Unknown	4
McBeth, John	East Nottingham	1
McCalla, Alexander	Charlestown	1
McCamant, James	West Nantmeal	1
McCaraher, Captain Alexander	Pikeland	2
McClenachan, John F.	Londonderry	1
McClure, Arthur	New London	2
McDowell, James	Oxford	5
McDowell, John	New London	2
McIlhenny, George	Charlestown	2
McIntire, Andrew	New Garden	1
McKinley, Alexander	Pikeland	4
McPherson, Agnes	Sadsbury	1
Menough, John	New London	1
Moore, David	West Nottingham	1
Moore, Dr. Joseph	Goshen	3
Moore, Hannah	Goshen	1
Moore, James	West Nantmeal	5
Moore, William, Esquire	Charlestown	10
Morrison, Alexander	New London	5
Nice, John	East Nantmeal	1
Park, Joseph, Esquire	Sadsbury	4
Phipps, Caleb	East Fallowfield	5
Piersol, Mordecai	West Nantmeal	1
Pinkerton, William	Oxford	2
Polk, William	West Nottingham	3
Potts, Thomas	Coventry	6
Power, John	East Nottingham	1
Power, Patrick	East Nottingham	8
Pritchard, Anthony	Charlestown	4
Reed, James	New London	3
Reed, William	New London	2
Richards, William	West Whiteland	3
Richardson, Richard	East Whiteland	5
Ross, John	Londongrove	1
Ruston, Job	Oxford	10
Scott, Thomas	Unknown	1
Shearer, William	New London	3
Shippen, Joseph, Jr.	Kennett	3
Sidwell, Lydia	East Nottingham	1
Skiles, Herman	West Caln	1

Name	Township	Number of Slaves Registered
Smith, Elizabeth	West Nottingham	1
Smith, John	New London	1
Smith, Margaret (Heirs of)	West Nottingham	1
Starrett, William	East Nantmeal	3
Starrett, William	Oxford	1
Steele, William	Unknown	2
Strawbridge, Joseph	Londonderry	1
Strawbridge, Thomas	Londonderry	3
Tanner, Philip	East Nottingham	2
Teales, John	East Fallowfield	2
Tenplin, Richard	East Nantmeal	1
Thomas, Benjamin	Charlestown	1
Trego, Moses	West Nantmeal	1
Vanlasey, John	Unknown	4
Vanleer, Branson	East Nantmeal	5
Wallace, Elizabeth	West Caln	2
Walters, Thomas	Tredyffrin	2
Wayne, General Anthony	Easttown	1
Wherry, David	East Nottingham	2
Whiting, John	London Britain	2
Wiley, Captain Thomas	Unknown	1
Wiley, David	Londongrove	3
Williams, Hugh	East Nantmeal	1
Williams, John	Tredyffrin	1
Wilson, David	Tredyffrin	1
Wilson, James	East Nottingham	1
Wilson, John	Tredyffrin	2
Totals: 142 Slaveholders	**Oxford (28 slaves)** **Charlestown (24)** **Tredyffrin (23)** **Londonderry (20)** **West Nantmeal (19)**	**470 slaves**

Appendix B. Chester County Underground Railroad Agents

NAME (N = 132) Variable indicates the individuals who were agents on Chester County's Underground Railroad. These include station masters, conductors and financiers. Names of agents identified in William Still's *Underground Railroad* (1872), and primary source documentation (letters, diaries and Proceedings of Progressive Friends) at Chester County Historical Society. Of the 132 agents 31 were African American (3 women & 28 men); and 101 were whites (27 women & 74 men).

AGE (N = 83) Variable indicates the age of the agent in 1850. *Federal Census of 1850* used as a source. Average age of agents was 44 years old.

RESIDENCE (N = 123) Variable indicates the Chester County Township or other city or county in which the agent resided in 1850. *Federal Census of 1850* used as a source. Highest concentrations in Chester County can be found in Kennett (22), West Chester (20) and Oxford (13). At least 10 of the 123 agents whose residence is known lived outside of the county in such places as Wilmington, Delaware (6), Lancaster County (2), and Philadelphia (1).

RELIGION (N = 107) Variable represents the denominational affiliation of agent. Taken from contemporary newspaper obituaries as well as church records. Of the 107 agents whose religion is known, the following breakdown has been identified: Quaker (82); Presbyterian (9); African Methodist Episcopalian (8); African Union Methodist Protestant (5); Episcopalian (2) and Baptist (1). The "L" indicates membership in the Longwood Progressive Friends Meeting, which was an interdenominational group. Of the 107 agents whose religion is known, 45 belonged to the Longwood Meeting.

WEALTH (N = 43) Variable represents the value of an agent's estate in 1850. Taken from *Chester County Tax Record for 1850*. Note that 14 of the agents were homemaker/spouses who would not possess any taxable estate. Population is so small that no conclusive statement can be reached on this variable.

OCCUPATION (N = 88) Variable indicates the occupation of the agent in 1850. Taken from *Federal Census of 1850*. Of the 88 agents whose occupation is known, the following breakdown has been identified: farmers (25); homemakers (14); ministers (9); tradesmen (8); physicians (7); teachers (6); merchants (5); politicians (3); scientists (2); other (9). The nature of these professions places the agents squarely in the middle-class.

REFORM (N = 31) Variable indicates the number and type of reform activity in which the agent was involved other than abolitionism. Taken from *Dictionary of Quaker Biography*, (manuscript copy at Quaker Collection, Haverford College Library), J. Smith Futhey & Gilbert Cope's History of Chester County (1881), and family genealogies at Chester County Historical Society. Of the 31 agents who were known to have reform involvements outside of abolitionism: 19 were involved in temperance (T); 17 in women's rights (WR); 7 in peace reforms (Pc); and 1 in prison reform (PR). Ten of the agents had multiple reform involvements outside of abolitionism.

POLITICAL AFFILIATION (N = 11) Variable indicates partisan affiliation of agent. Taken from Futhey & Cope's *History of Chester County* (1881) and family genealogies at Chester County Historical Society. Population is so small as to prevent any conclusions.

KINSHIP (N = 51) Variable indicates familial or professional relationship with at least one other agent. Taken from family genealogies at Chester County Historical Society. m = married to; s = sibling of; ch = child of; p = parent of; r = relative of; a = association with.

NOTE: Black agents listed in italics.

Name	Life dates	Age / 1850	Residence	Religion	Wealth	Occupt'n	Reforms	Political	Kinship
Agnew, Allen			Kennett	Presbytn.	$5,854	farmer	T		m. Maria
Agnew, Maria	1810-1870	40	Kennett	Presbytn.		homemaker			m. Allen
Amos, James	*1824-1864*	*26*	*Oxford*	*Presbytn.*		*minister*			*s. Thom.*
Amos, Thomas	*1826-1869*	*24*	*Oxford*	*Presbytn.*		*minister*			*s. James*
Barnard, Eusebius	1801-1865	49	Pocopson	Quaker / L	$6,041	minister	WR		m. Sarah M.
Barnard, Sarah D.	1809-1881	41	E. Marlbor	Quaker / L		homemaker			m. Simon
Barnard, Sarah M.	1819-1887	31	Pocopson	Quaker / L		homemaker			m. Eus.
Barnard, Simon	1802-1886	48	E. Marlbor	Quaker / L	$5,646	farmer			m. Sarah D.
Barnard, Vincent	1813-1858	37	Kennett	Quaker / L		botanist			
Barnard, William	18??-1864		Pocopson	Quaker / L	$3,535	farmer			
Bonsall, Thomas	1797-?	53	W. Caln	Presbytn.	$7,815	farmer			
Borton, Beulah	18??-1881		Kennett	Quaker / L		homemaker			
Borton, Thomas	1794-1868	56	Kennett	Quaker / L					
Brosius, Daniel	17??-1847		Kennett	Quaker		potter			ch. Mah/s. Ed
Brosius, Edwin	1832-1885	18	Kennett	Quaker	$715	potter		Repub.	ch. Mah/s. Dan
Brosius, Mahlon	1797-1863	53	U. Oxford	Quaker		potter/farmer			p. Ed/Dan/m.
Brosius, Mary			U. Oxford	Quaker		homemaker			m. Mah/2 sons
Brown, John A.	*1799-1877*	*51*	*W. Chester*	*AME*		*minister*			
Brown. Thomas			*W. Chester*						
Burleigh, Cyrus M.				Quaker / L			T		
Cain, Augustus W			Sadsbury			physician			
Chapman, George				Quaker / L					
Coates, Ann				Quaker / L					
Cope, Caleb S.	1736-1824		Quaker						
Cox, Hannah	1797-1876	53	Kennett	Quaker / L		homemaker	T, WR, PR		m. John
Cox, John			Kennett	Quaker / L	$7,289	farmer			m. Hannah
Countee, Dave			*Uwchlan*						
Craige, Harry			*Wilm., DE*						
Darlington, Hannah			W Chester	Quaker / L	$1,200		WR		
Dugdale, Jos. A.	1810-1896	40	Kennett	Quaker / L		minister	T, WR, Pc		m. Ruth
Dugdale, Ruth			Kennett	Quaker / L					
Dugdale, Sarah B.			Quaker / L						
Eshelman, J.K.			Downtwn			physician			
Evans, David	1813-1898	37	Willistown	Quaker	$4,712	teach/farm			
Everhart, William	1785-1868	65	W Chester	Presbytn	$26,252	judge/US Cong		Whig	
Freeman, Benj.	*1800-1883*	*50*	*W Chester*	*AME*	*$800*	*teamster*			
Fulton, Ann				Quaker / L					
Fulton, Esther			Sadsbury	Presbyterian		homemaker			m.Joseph
Fulton, James Jr.	1812-1850	38	E. Fallowfield	Quaker	$1,565	farmer	T		
Fulton, Joseph	1821-1887	29	Sadsbury	Presbytn		farmer		Repub.	m. Esther
Fussell, Barthol.	1794-1871	56	Kennett	Quaker / L	$3,000	physician	T, WR		m. Lydia
Fussell, Edwin	1813-1882	37	W Vincent	Quaker		physician			
Fussell, Lydia	17??-1841		Kennett	Quaker / L		homemaker			m. Barth.
Fussell, William	1786-1856	64	W Vincent	Quaker					
Garrett, Isaac	1798-1870	52	Willistown	Quaker	$6,570	farmer			s. Thomas
Garrett, Thomas	1789-1871	61	Wilm., DE	Quaker / L		merchant			s. Isaac
George, John	1815-1896	35	W Chester		$1,500	tailor	T, WR, Pc		
Glasgow, Samuel	*1803-1876*	*47*	*Oxford*	*AME*	*$350*	*brickmaker*			
Hannum, Enoch S.	1820-1906	30	New London	Quaker / L		minister			
Hambleton,Alice E.	17??-1866		U Oxford	Quaker / L		homemaker			m. Charles
Hambleton, Charles			U Oxford	Quaker					m. Alice
Hamilton, Joseph			*Wilm., DE*						
Hanway, Castner	1821-1893	29	Cochranv.	Quaker/L					r. S. Pennock
Hayes, Esther	1790-1897	60	Newlin			homemaker			m. Mordecai
Hayes, Mordecai			Newlin						m. Esther
Hinson, Emory	*1792-1852*	*58*	*Oxford*	*AUMP*		*farmer*			

Name	Life dates	Age / 1850	Residence	Religion	Wealth	Occupt'n	Reforms	Political	Kinship
Ivins, Barclay				Quaker / L					
James, Ebenezer				Quaker / L					
Johnson, Severen			*Wilm., DE*						
Kent, Benjamin	1805-1881	45	W Grove	Quaker		minister	T		m. Hannah
Kent, Hannah	1805-1882	45	W Grove	Quaker		homemaker			m. Benjamin
Kimber, Emmor	1774-1850	76	Kimberton	Quaker		teacher			
Lamborn, Jonathan	1778-?	72	Kennett	Quaker / L	$3,296				
Lamborn, Rachel	1824-1894	26	Kennett	Quaker		teacher	Pc		m. Rob/sis H. Cox
Lamborn, Robert	1791-?	59	Kennett	Quaker	$11,000	farmer	T		m. Rachel
Lee, Henry				*Sadsbury*					
Lewis, Elizabeth			W Vincent	Quaker			WR, T		ch. John/s. Gr, ME
Lewis, Enoch S.	1776-1856	74	W Vincent	Quaker	$3,055	teach/farm			p. Gr. ME, Eliz, Mar.
Lewis, Graceanna	1821-1912	29	W Vincent	Quaker		naturalist	WR, T		ch. John/s. ME, Eliz
Lewis, Mariann			W Vincent	Quaker			WR, T		ch. John/s. Gr, Eliz
Lindley, Jacob	1744-1814	N/A	Avondale	Quaker		minister			
Maris, Norris	1803-1893	47	W Vincent	Quaker		farmer	T	Repub.	
Mendenh'l, Dinah	1807-1889	43	Kennett	Quaker / L		homemaker	WR		m. Isaac
Mendenh'l, Isaac	1807-1882	43	Kennett	Quaker / L	$14,884		T, WR		m. Dinah
Meredith, Isaac	1802-?	48	Newlin	Quaker / L	$11,000	farmer	WR		m. Thomazine
Meredith, James	1769-?	81	Newlin	Quaker / L			Pc		
Meredith Thomazine	1812-1894	38	Newlin	Quaker / L		homemaker			m. Isaac
Moore, Charles	1823-1892	27	Uwchlan	Quaker		farmer		Dem.	
Moore, Esther				Quaker / L					
Munson, Comegys			*Wilm., DE*						
Painter, James	1792-1867	58	W Chester	Quaker / L	$5,850				
Painter, Samuel M.	1809-1884	41	W Chester	Quaker	$3,300	lumber merch		Repub.	
Parker, William	*1824-187?*	*26*	*Lancaster*	*AME*		*farmer*			
Paxson, Jacob L.	1797-1890	53	W Chester	Quaker / L					
Peart, Louis	1808-1882	42	Tredyffrin			farmer			
Pennock, Jesse	17??-1863		E Marlbor	Quaker / L	$3,428		Pc		
Pennock, Mary J.	1791-1866	59	Kennett	Quaker / L			WR		m. Moses
Pennock, Moses	1786-1860	64	Kennett	Quaker / L	$4,196	farm/mech	T		m. Mary
Pennock, Samuel	1816-1903	34	Kennett	Quaker	$3,000	industr'list	WR	Repub.	
Pennyp'kr, Elijah F.	1804-1888	46	Schuylkill	Quaker	$4,660	PA legis.	T	Repub.	
Philips, Owen			E. Nantmeal	Baptist					
Pierce, Gideon	1793-1877	57	E Fallowfield	Quaker	$2,285	lumber merch			
Preston, Amos			London Gr	Quaker / L	$4,835	farmer			p. Dr. Ann
Preston, Ann	1813-1872	37	W Grove	Quaker		physician	T, WR		r. Dr. B Fuss.
Price, Benjamin	1793-1871	57	W Chester	Quaker		teacher			p. Isaiah
Price, Isaiah	1822-1901	28	W Chester	Quaker		dentist			ch. Benj.
Price, Jacob	1826-1905	24	W Chester	Quaker		physician			ch. Jane & Benj.
Price, Jane	1791-1876	59	W Chester	Quaker		homemaker			m. Benj.
Price, John	*1821-1890*	*29*	*W Chester*	*AME*					
Pyle, Benjamin	1819-1887	31	W Chester	Episc / L	$900	lawyer	T	Repub.	
Richards, Henry			*Schuylkill*			*farmer*			
Robinson, Elizabeth			*Uwchlan*						
Robinson, Joshua			*Uwchlan*						
Schofield, Fannie			Sadsbury	Quaker / L					
Shadd, Abraham	*1801-?*	*49*	*W Chester*	*AME*	*$3,000*	*shoemaker*			
Shadd, Mary Ann	*1823-1842*	*27*	*W Chester*	*AME*		*teacher*			
Sharples, Philip P.	1810-1902	40	W Chester		$12,320	Brickmaker			
Smith, John			*W Chester*						
Speakman, Micajah	1781-1852	69	W Nantmeal	Quaker	$9,181	farmer			
Speakman, William	1808-1892	42	Uwchlan	Quaker		postmaster			
Stebbins, Sumner	1809-1884	41	E Marlbor	Quaker / L		physician	T	Repub.	a. Dr. Benj. Fussell

Name	Life dates	Age / 1850	Residence	Religion	Wealth	Occupt'n	Reforms	Political	Kinship
Still, William	*1821-1902*	*29*	*Phila.*	*AME*		*clerk PAS*			
Taylor, Enoch L.			E. Fallow.	Quaker / L	$2,300	farmer			
Taylor, George	1803-1891	47	New Gard.	Quaker		Free Pro mer	WR, Pc		a. E. Lewis
Thomas, Zebulon	1781-1865	69	E Caln		$2,580	lawyer			
Thorne, J. William			Sadsbury						
Trimble, William I	1823-1897	27	W. Whiteland	Quaker	$1,880	miller			
Tubman, Harriet	*1821-1913*	*29*	*New York*						
Vickers, John	17??-1860		Lionville	Quaker		farm/potter			
Walker, James	*1800-?*	*50*	*Kennett*		*$1,072*	*laborer*			
Walls, Albert	*1834-1863*	*16*	*Oxford*	*AUMP*		*farmer*			
Walls, Edward	*1793-1880*	*57*	*Oxford*	*AUMP*	*$462*	*farmer*			*s. Geo, Wm*
Walls, George	*1805-1884*	*44*	*Oxford*	*AUMP*	*$3,910*	*farmer*			*s. Ed, Wm*
Walls, William	*1801-1854*	*49*	*Oxford*	*AUMP*	*$134*	*farmer*			*s. Ed, Geo*
Webb, Edward	1819-1898	31	Oxford	Presby/ L		minister	WR		
Webb, William	1819-1891	31	E Marlbor	Quaker / L	$5,443				
Whitson, Thomas	1828-1907	22	Lancaster	Quaker		farmer	Pc	Repub.	
Williams, Isaac				*Concord*					
Wilmer, George				*Wilm., DE*					
Wilson, Ephraim			London Gr	Quaker / L	$8,100	farmer			
Worthington, John T.	1801-1869	49	W Chester	Episcopal	$11,910	Judge			
Wright, John			*Willistown*						
TOTALS									
N = 132		**N = 83**	**N = 123**	**N = 107**	**N = 43**	**N = 88**	**N = 31**	**N = 11**	**N = 51**

Appendix C.
Chester Countians
in the 54th Massachusetts Regiment

NAME	CO.	AGE	OCCUPATION	HOME	TERMINATION OF SERVICE *(killed or wounded at Fort Wagner)*
Anderson, James	G	33	laborer	Chester Co.	wounded / Aug 20, '65
Anderson John	D	27	shoemaker	West Chester	August 20, 1865
Anderson, Solomon	B	34	farmer	West Chester	June 7, 1865
Berry, Samuel	A	23	farmer	West Chester	July 16, 1864
Blake, Lemuel	B	21	farmer	West Chester	June 7, 1865
Brown, George	B	20	farmer	West Chester	August 20, 1865
Brown, Jesse H.	B	23	farmer	West Chester	wounded & imprisoned
Brown, Morris	B	22	wagoner	West Chester	killed
Clark, Andrew	D	30	farmer	Chester Co.	killed
Cole James	B	19	farmer	Oxford	wounded / Aug. 20, 1865
Cole, Josiah	B	19	farmer	Coatesville	August 20, 1865
Cooper, Thomas F.	B	26	laborer	West Chester	wounded
Counsel, George	B	26	laborer	West Chester	June 7, 1865
Dixon, John W.	B	22	farmer	West Chester	Sept. 1, 1865
Douglass, John	B	23	farmer	Unionville	August 20, 1865
Farmer, George	B	30	farmer	Unionville	August 20, 1865
Glasgow, Abraham	B	26	farmer	Unionville	wounded
Glasgow, London	B	22	farmer	Unionville	killed
Hazard, Solomon	B	22	farmer	West Chester	wounded / Aug. 20, 1865
Henson, John	C	20	laborer	Coatesville	August 20, 1865
Hercules, Lewis	B	21	farmer	West Chester	April 24, 1864
Jay, George	B	19	farmer	Oxford	August 20, 1865
Jay, Wesley	B	26	farmer	Oxford	August 20, 1865
Jay, William	B	22	farmer	Oxford	August 20, 1865
Johnson, Clayton	B	18	farmer	West Chester	August 20, 1865
Jones, Joseph	C	19	farmer	Coatesville	August 20, 1865

Name	Co.	Age	Occupation	Home	Termination of service *(killed or wounded at Fort Wagner)*
Jones, William	K	22	farmer	West Chester	died of disease
Lloyd, Thomas	D	20	farmer	Chester Co.	killed
Merriman, George F.	B	22	farmer	West Chester	died of wound
Parker, Jeremiah	B	23	farmer	West Chester	August 20, 1865
Pennington, William F.	C	18	farmer	Coatesville	August 20, 1865
Preston, Charles H.	B	22	farmer	West Chester	August 20, 1865
Rigby, William	B	21	farmer	West Chester	August 20, 1865
Rudolph, Francis J.	K	19	farmer	West Chester	August 20, 1865
Seaman, Alfred B.	G	25	laborer	Parkesburg	Sept. 28, 1865
Shirley, John	B	23	farmer	West Chester	August 20, 1865
Smith, Edward H.	B	21	farmer	West Chester	August 20, 1865
Smith, John	C	18	farmer	Coatesville	August 20, 1865
Smith, Richard R.	K	22	farmer	Unionville	August 20, 1865
Spriggs, Enos	B	21	farmer	West Chester	August 20, 1865
Vanleer, George R.	B	21	farmer	West Chester	deserted May 1863
Walls, Albert	B	29	farmer	Oxford	killed
Washington, Stephen	B	27	laborer	West Chester	August 20, 1865
Washington, William H.	B	21	laborer	West Chester	August 20, 1865
Williams, Henry B.	I	18	farmer	Chester Co.	killed
Wilson, Samuel R.	B	21	farmer	West Chester	killed

Appendix D. Chester Countians *in the* U.S. Colored Troops

Name	Co.	Age	Occupation	Home	Termination of service
3rd Regiment					
Adams, Richard	A	63		West Marlborough	
Anderson, Jacob H.	B	18	laborer	New London	
Brown, George A.	B			West Chester	
Davis, Samuel C.	A			Lower Oxford	
Glasgow, John	C			East Nottingham	Died: January 16, 1865
Hardy, James J.	H			West Chester	
Hardy, Samuel	H	19	farm laborer	Westtown	
Harley, Henry	B			Sadsbury	
Harrod, James H.	G	24	laborer	East Fallowfield	
Henry, Thomas	B			West Chester	
Kelly, Samuel	G	25	laborer	West Chester	
Mayhew, Samuel	E			New London	Died: Sept. 1, 1863
Melton, Joseph	B			West Chester	Discharged: June 11, 1865
Miller, Wesley	B		farm laborer	East Bradford	
Peach, George	A		fiddler	East Marlborough	Deserted: Feb. 16, 1865
Raymond, James S.	B			Pennsbury	
Richards, John H.	A			West Chester	
Richardson, John	H	23	laborer	West Goshen	
Tinson, Peter	B	20	farm laborer	Exton	
Valentine, Tillman	B			Pennsbury	
Walker, James	D		farm laborer	Pocopson	
Walker, William	D	25	farm laborer	Pocopson	
Williams, Allison	B			West Chester	
Wilson, George J.	C	29	farm laborer	Lower Oxford	Died: Sept. 16, 1863
Young, Alfred J.	G			East Fallowfield	Discharged: Jan. 26, 1865

Name	Co.	Age	Occupation	Home	Termination of service
6th Regiment					
Boggs, James	D	41	farm laborer	West Caln	
Brown, John W.	A	23	laborer	West Chester	
Carson, William	C	36	farm laborer	Pocopson	
Chew, Richard H.	F			Thornbury	
Elsey, William P.	G			West Bradford	
Golden, Charles	H			Lionville	Killed: July 10, 1864
Gover, Richard	C	26	farm laborer	Pocopsin	
Hammond, Jacob	D	24	iron worker	East Brandywine	Died: August 21, 1865
Henson, Lewis J.	A			Valley	
Hopkins, Daniel	A			Valley	
Irons, David H.	A			East Whiteland	Discharged: May 16, 1865
Johns, William	E			West Brandywine	
Johnson, Henry	A	22		West Chester	Discharged: Aug. 30, 1864
Jones, George H.	A	21	laborer	Valley	
Jones, Isaac W.	A			Valley	
Jones, Nathan C.	A			West Chester	
Lewis, Charles	C			East Brandywine	
Loper, Nehemiah	A			West Chester	
Miller, Israel W.	A	25	farm laborer	East Brandywine	Died: July 16, 1865
Miller, John	D	20	laborer	West Caln	
Miller, Lassing	A			Valley	Died: September 1865
Miller, William	D			West Caln	
Price, Marshall	C	28	farm laborer	East Fallowfield	
Richmond, Peter	D	29	laborer	West Goshen	Died: Dec. 5, 1864
Shin, Amos	B	25	laborer	Highland	Killed: Sept. 29, 1864
Skeere, Henry I.	C	26	farm laborer	Birmingham	Killed: Sept. 29, 1864
Smith, William H.	F	26	farm laborer	Westtown	
Vance, Joseph	B	29	laborer	Kennett Square	
8th Regiment					
Coursey, Thomas	B			Valley	
Hercules, Gilbert S.	A			South Coventry	
Johnson, Charles	B			Valley	Killed: Feb. 20, 1864
Lewis, Elija	F	27	farmer	Willistown	
Miller, Josephus	D			Sadsbury	Discharged: Jan. 3, 1865
Thomas, Franklin	A	35	farm laborer	East Whiteland	Died: March 1, 1864
22nd Regiment					
Woodyard, Hiram	K			East Whiteland	
25th Regiment					
Nixon, James J.	K			West Chester	Died: June 9, 1864
Nixon, Solomon E.	K	16	farm laborer	East Caln	Died: Sept. 23, 1864

Name	Co.	Age	Occupation	Home	Termination of service
32nd Regiment					
Brice, Samuel	G	31	farm laborer	Newlin	
Conner, Charles	B			East Marlborough	
Cooper, Solomon	D	44	laborer	West Chester	Died: 1865
Harley, Charles	F			Sadsbury	
Johnson, William R.	H			West Chester	
Ray, Samuel	E	43	farm laborer	Kennett	
Raymond, Benjamin	I	18	farm laborer	Pennsbury	
Wilmer, Edward	B			Unionville	
41st Regiment					
Bell, William S.	D			West Goshen	
Green, Cornelius	B	28	laborer	Valley	
Mitchell, Levi H.	B			Downingtown	
43rd Regiment					
Winters, Isaac J.	F		farmer	Westtown	
45th Regiment					
Brown, William	I			Marshallton	
Gover, Samuel				East Brandywine	Died: June 29, 1865
Lloyd, John	I			East Fallowfield	
Hamilton, Thomas	I			West Chester	
127th Regiment					
Carter, Joseph	F			Kennett	Discharged: Oct. 20, 1865
Hallager, David	C				
Ringold, Wilmer	F	21	farm laborer	Lower Oxford	Discharged: Oct. 20, 1865

Lenders *to the* Exhibition

The American Numismatic Society, New York City
The Atwater Kent Museum, Philadelphia
Dr. Charles Butler, past president, Coatesville NAACP
The Historical Society of Delaware, Wilmington
Christopher Densmore
Friends Historical Library of Swarthmore College
Grand Illusions Clothing Company, Newark, Delaware
The Langston Hughes Memorial Library Archives, Lincoln University, Pennsylvania
Illinois State Historical Library, Springfield
State Historical Society of Iowa, Des Moines
The Lancaster County Historical Society
Moores Memorial Library, Christiana, Pennsylvania
National Archives of Canada, Ottawa
National Portrait Gallery, Smithsonian Institution, Washington, D.C.
The Historical Society of Pennsylvania, Philadelphia
State Museum of Pennsylvania, Pennsylvania Historical and Museum Commission, Harrisburg
The Philadelphia Museum of Art
J. Justin and Gwen Ragsdale
The Rochester Museum & Science Center, Rochester, New York
The Bayard Rustin Fund, New York City
Stargazers Winery, Coatesville, Pennsylvania
Dane Tilghman
The D.B. Weldon Library, University of Western Ontario
West Chester NAACP - Doris Bond, president
Wilmington Friends School

Checklist *of the* Exhibition

1. **Thomas Garrett**
Bass Otis (1784-1861)
Oil on canvas
30 x 25 in. (1838)
Historical Society of Delaware
Wilmington, Delaware

2. **Harriet Tubman**
Robert Savon Pious (1908-1983)
Oil on canvas
12 3/16 x 9 5/8 in. (1951)
National Portrait Galley, Smithsonian Institution;
Gift of the Harmon Foundation
Washington D.C.

3. **William Still**
Dane Tilghman (1957 -)
Acrylic on paper
20 x 25 in. (2001)
Chester County Historical Society

4. **Frederick Douglass**
Freeman Thorpe (1844 - 1922)
Oil on canvas
37 x 32 in. (1896)
State Historical Society of Iowa
Des Moines, Iowa

5. **Lucretia Mott**
Carte-de-visite by H.C. Phillips
Philadelphia (ca. 1860-66)
Pierce Lamborn Collection
Chester County Historical Society

6. **William Lloyd Garrison**
Carte-de-visite by Lothrop
Boston, Massachusetts (ca. 1860-68)
Pierce Lamborn Collection
Chester County Historical Society

7. **Slave badge**
"Charleston / No. 112 / Porter / 1815"
Copper (1815)
The American Numismatic Society
New York, New York

8. **Free black badge**
"City of Charleston / Free"
Copper alloy (ca. 1848-1860)
The American Numismatic Society
New York, New York

9. **Reynold's Political Map of the United States**
Hand-colored print (1856)
The Atwater Kent Museum
Philadelphia, Pennsylvania

10. **Diagram of slave ship**
Lithograph
Langston Hughes Memorial Library Archives,
Lincoln University
Lincoln University, Pennsylvania

11. **"Inventory document"**
signed John Morton
Manuscript
Chester County Archives

12. **Will**
signed by Margery Baker
Manuscript (June 3, 1773)
Chester County Archives

13. **"Damage claim"**
Manuscript (1782)
Chester County Archives

14. **Hand shackles**
used in middle passage
Iron (late eighteenth century)
J. Justin and Gwen Ragsdale
Philadelphia, Pennsylvania

15. **Adult hand shackles**
Iron (early nineteenth century)
J. Justin and Gwen Ragsdale
Philadelphia, Pennsylvania

16. **Child's hand shackles**
Iron (early nineteenth century)
J. Justin and Gwen Ragsdale
Philadelphia, Pennsylvania

17. **Branding iron**
Iron, wood (early nineteenth century)
J. Justin and Gwen Ragsdale
Philadelphia, Pennsylvania

18. **Bowl**
Wood (early nineteenth century)
J. Justin and Gwen Ragsdale
Philadelphia, Pennsylvania

19. **Slave harness**
Iron, brass (late eighteenth century)
Historical Society of Pennsylvania (1000.1214)
Philadelphia, Pennsylvania

20. **Gordon, runaway slave**
Photograph (ca. 1863)
Illinois State Historical Library
Springfield, Illinois

21. **Slave tombstone**
Earthenware (early nineteenth century)
J. Justin and Gwen Ragsdale
Philadelphia, Pennsylvania

22. **Surveyor's compass**
Brass, glass, wood, iron
(mid-eighteenth century)
Made by Benjamin Chandlee (1723-1791)
Chester County Historical Society

23. **"Slave registry for Chester County"**
Manuscript, transcription of
1780 document
Chester County Historical Society

24. **"Fugitive slave claim"**
Manuscript (August 10, 1836)
signed by William Price
Chester County Archives

25. **Longwood Progressive Friends Meeting House**
Albumen photograph by J.W. Hurn
Philadelphia, Pennsylvania (ca. 1865)
Chester County Historical Society

26. **Bench**
Longwood Progressive Friends
Meeting House
Painted pine (mid-nineteenth century)
Gift of Longwood Friends Meeting
Chester County Historical Society

27. **Goshen Friends Meeting**
Photograph by Gilbert Cope (1889)
Chester County Historical Society

28. **"Journal of David Evans"**
Manuscript (1838 to 1890s)
Chester County Historical Society

29. **Bethel AME Church**
West Chester, Pennsylvania
Albumen photograph (1880)
Chester County Historical Society

30. **Hosanna African Union Methodist Protestant Church**
Photographer unidentified
Chester County Historical Society

31. **Frederick Douglass**
Daguerreotype (ca. 1848)
Albert Cook Myers Collection
Chester County Historical Society

32. **"Independence Day Address"**
Manuscript, Frederick Douglass (1852)
Rochester Museum & Science Center
Rochester, New York

33. **"Lectures on American Slavery"**
Manuscript, Frederick Douglass
Rochester Museum & Science Center
Rochester, New York

34. **Ashmun Institute**
Drawing (ca. 1854)
Langston Hughes Memorial Library Archives, Lincoln University
Lincoln University, Pennsylvania

35. **John M. Dickey**
Oil on canvas (ca. 1854)
33 x 38 in.
Langston Hughes Memorial Library Archives, Lincoln University
Lincoln University, Pennsylvania

36. **Bible**
Owned by John M. Dickey (1830)
Langston Hughes Memorial Library Archives, Lincoln University
Lincoln University, Pennsylvania

37. **"Foundation of Ashmun Institute"**
Manuscript (1853)
Langston Hughes Memorial Library Archives, Lincoln University
Lincoln University, Pennsylvania

38. **"Constitution of Chester County Colonization Society"**
Manuscript (ca. 1830-35)
Chester County Historical Society

39. **"Declaration of the Anti-Slavery Convention"**
Manuscript (Dec. 4, 1833)
Philadelphia, Pennsylvania
Chester County Historical Society

40. **"Declaration of the Anti-Slavery Convention" handkerchief**
Silk (ca. 1833)
Chester County Historical Society

41. **"Negro Woman Who Sittest Pining in Captivity . . ." purse**
Silk, cotton (mid-nineteenth century)
Chester County Historical Society

42. **"Letter to Hannah Darlington, signed by Ann Preston"**
Manuscript (July 3, 1847)
Chester County Historical Society

43. **John Vickers**
Engraving (ca. 1854)
Chester County Historical Society

44. **Dish painted by John Vickers**
Ironstone (1824)
Gift of Henry F. duPont
Chester County Historical Society

45. **Flowerpot made by John Vickers**
Redware (1850-1860)
Chester County Historical Society

46. **Hannah Cox**
Carte-de-visite by H.C. Phillips, Philadelphia, Pennsylvania (ca. 1865-66)
Peirce-Lamborn Collection
Chester County Historical Society

47. **John Cox**
Carte-de-visite by H.C. Phillips, Philadelphia, Pennsylvania (ca. 1865-66)
Peirce-Lamborn Collection
Chester County Historical Society

48. **Isaac Mendenhall**
Carte-de-visite by H.C. Phillips, Philadelphia, Pennsylvania (1869)
Peirce-Lamborn Collection
Chester County Historical Society

49. **Dinah Mendenhall**
Carte-de-visite by H.C. Phillips, Philadelphia, Pennsylvania (1869)
Peirce-Lamborn Collection
Chester County Historical Society

50. **Oakdale, Kennett Square, Pennsylvania**
Photograph, by Marie L. Hughes (1975)
Chester County Historical Society

51. **Spring House at Oakdale**
Photograph, by Marie L. Hughes (1975)
Chester County Historical Society

52. **Barn at Oakdale**
Photograph, by Marie L. Hughes (1975)
Chester County Historical Society

53. **Cox Homestead, Kennett Square, Pennsylvania**
Photograph, photographer unidentified, (ca. 1910)
Chester County Historical Society

54. **Graceanna Lewis**
Photographer unidentified
Chester County Historical Society

55. **Sunnyside, Kimberton, Pennsylvania**
Photograph, by Wayne E. Homan (1975)
Chester County Historical Society

56. **Tea Service of Thomas Garrett**
Silver, Reed & Barton
Taunton, Massachusetts (1866)
Historical Society of Delaware
Wilmington, Delaware

57. **Mary Ann Shadd Carey**
Halftone, photographer unidentified (1845-1855)
National Archives of Canada (NegC-029977)

58. **Abraham Shadd**
Photograph, photographer unidentified
The D.B. Weldon Library,
University of Western Ontario
London, Ontario, Canada

59. **Christiana Resistance**
Engraving taken from William Still,
Underground Railroad, 1872

60. **Survivors of Christiana Resistance**
Photograph, by William S. Gleim (ca. 1890)
Moores Memorial Library
Christiana, Pennsylvania

61. **Ruins of Christiana Resistance**
Photograph, by Gilbert Cope, October 24, 1896
Chester County Historical Society

62. **Corn cutter**
Oak, iron, mid-nineteenth century
Lancaster County Historical Society
Lancaster, Pennsylvania

63. **"A Voice from Harper's Ferry"**
Manuscript, by Osborne Perry Anderson (1873)
Chester County Historical Society

64. **"Commonwealth of Pennsylvania v. Amos B. McFarlan and Solomon States"**
Manuscript, indictment paper (July 1849)
Chester County Archives

65. **"Court of Quarter Sessions Papers"**
Manuscript, bail for Amos B. McFarlan, (July 1849)
Chester County Archives

66. **"Commonwealth of Pennsylvania v. Solomon States"**
Manuscript, recognizance for Solomon States (July 1849)
Chester County Archives

67. **William Still**
Engraving, by John Sartian, Philadelphia
Taken from William Still,
Underground Railroad, 1872
Chester County Historical Society

68. **"Underground Railroad"**
by William Still (1872)
Chester County Historical Society

69. **"Resurrection of Henry 'Box' Brown"**
Engraving
Taken from William Still,
Underground Railroad, 1872
Chester County Historical Society

70. **Passmore Williamson in Moyemensing Prison**
Daguerreotype, photographer unidentified, (1855)
Chester County Historical Society

71. **Visitor's Book for Passmore Williamson**
Manuscript (1855)
Chester County Historical Society

72. **Rescue of Jane Johnson**
Engraving taken from William Still,
Underground Railroad, 1872
Chester County Historical Society

73. **Banner of Abraham Lincoln's 1860 Presidential Campaign**
Silk (1860)
Chester County Historical Society

74. **Model bust of Abraham Lincoln**
Painted plaster, William Marshall Swayne (1828-1918)
(1870)
Chester County Historical Society

75. **Statue of Abraham Lincoln**
Painted plaster, William Marshall Swayne (1828-1918)
(ca. 1866)
Chester County Historical Society

76. **Lincoln Building**
Photograph, by Ned Goode (1958)
Chester County Historical Society

77. **"Proceedings, Pennsylvania Yearly Meeting of Progressive Friends"**
Manuscript (1862)
Friends Historical Library, Swarthmore College
Swarthmore, Pennsylvania

78. **"Memorial to President Lincoln"**
Manuscript, 1862
Friends Historical Library, Swarthmore College
Swarthmore, Pennsylvania

79. **"Colored Men Wanted"**
Manuscript (June 20, 1863)
Chester County Historical Society

80. **Badge**
54th Massachusetts Regiment
Silver, brass (ca. 1864)
State Museum of Pennsylvania,
Pennsylvania Historical and Museum Commission
Harrisburg, Pennsylvania

81. **Unidentified Black Soldier**
Carte-de-visite (between 1864-1866)
Chester County Historical Society

82. **Christian Fleetwood**
Photograph (ca. 1864)
Langston Hughes Memorial Library Archives,
Lincoln University
Lincoln University, Pennsylvania

83. **Rifle of Christian Fleetwood**
Iron, wood (mid-nineteenth century)
Langston Hughes Memorial Library Archives,
Lincoln University
Lincoln University, Pennsylvania

84. **Elks Fraternal Pin**
Brass (late twentieth century)
Gift of Renee Boyd
Chester County Historical Society

85. **Moses Hepburn**
Halftone from "West Chester Past & Present, Centennial Souvenir," published by *Daily Local News* (1899)
Chester County Historical Society

86. **Mr. Prejudice**
Horace Pippen (1888-1946)
Oil on canvas, 18" x 14" (1943)
The Philadelphia Museum of Art
Gift of Dr. & Mrs. Matthew Moore

87. **Springtime in 1892**
Ida Jones (1874-1959)
Oil on board, 22.875" x 28.875" (1952)
Chester County Historical Society

88. **Mechanical doll**
Metal, silk, wool, glass (1870-1889)
The Thura Truax Memorial Collection
Chester County Historical Society

89. **"Pickaninny" doll**
Cotton, Arnold Print Works (ca. 1892)
Chester County Historical Society

90. **"Darkey" doll**
Cotton, Cocheco Mfg. Co. (maker)
Ida A. Gutshell (designer) (ca. 1893)
Gift of Maxine Waldron
Chester County Historical Society

91. **Ku Klux Klan hood and robe**
Cotton (early twentieth century)
Chester County Historical Society

92. **Crowd gathering the morning after Walker lynching**
Photograph, by Joseph W. Belt
(August 1911)
Chester County Historical Society

93. **"Letter"**
Signed by "Robert" to Judge Butler
Manuscript, St. Joseph, Missouri
(August 23, 1911)
Chester County Archives

94. **"Pennegar and Lynching"**
Manuscript (1914)
Chester County Historical Society

95. **Ku Klux Klan march in West Chester, Pennsylvania**
Photograph, by Sarah Wesley
(January 12, 1991)
Chester County Historical Society

96. **"Constitution and by-laws of NAACP"**
Manuscript (November 1953)
Doris A. Bond
West Chester, Pennsylvania

97. **NAACP flag**
Polyester (ca. 1995)
Doris A. Bond
West Chester, Pennsylvania

98. **NAACP pin**
Tin (1977)
Chester County Historical Society
Gift of Renee Byrd

99. **"How the NAACP began"**
Manuscript, by Mary W. Ovington (1914)
Dr. Charles H. Butler
Coatesville, Pennsylvania

100. **"Letter authorizing the charter of West Chester NAACP"**
Manuscript, signed Gloster B. Current,
(May 20, 1955)
Doris A. Bond
West Chester, Pennsylvania

101. **"Letter to West Chester School Superintendent, Dr. G. Arthur Stetson"**
Manuscript, signed by Charles A. Melton,
President of West Chester NAACP,
(August 29, 1955)
Doris A. Bond
West Chester, Pennsylvania

102. **"Letter to West Chester NAACP on school desegregation efforts"**
Manuscript (June 27, 1955)
signed by Dr. G. Arthur Stetson
Doris A. Bond
West Chester, Pennsylvania

103. **Bayard Rustin and the Reverend Dr. Martin Luther King, Jr.**
Photograph, by Burt Smith (1965)
Bayard Rustin Foundation
New York, New York

104. **School Vouchers**
Manuscript (June 1, 1830)
Wilmington, Delaware
Wilmington Friends School
Wilmington, Delaware

105. **Regimental Flag, 54th Massachusetts**
Cotton swath (1863)
Christopher Densmore
West Chester, Pennsylvania

Suggestions *for* Further Reading

Anderson, Jervis. *Bayard Rustin: Troubles I've Seen.* New York: Harper Collins, 1997.

Anderson, Osborne Perry. *A Voice From Harper's Ferry.* Washington D.C.: J.D. Enos, 1878.

Bacon, Margret Hope. *Valiant Friend: The Life of Lucretia Mott.* New York: Walker, 1980.

Bassuk, Daniel. *Abraham Lincoln and the Quakers.* Wallingford, PA: Pendle Hill, 1987.

Blassingame, John W. *The Slave Community. Plantation Life in the Antebellum South.* New York: Oxford University, 1978.

Blockson, Charles L. *The Underground Railroad in Pennsylvania.* Jacksonville, FL: Flame International, 1981.

Bradford, Sarah. *Harriet Tubman: The Moses of Her People (1886)* reprinted by Applewood Books, Bedford, MA, 1993.

Bradley, John. *Around the Oak: Oxford, Pennsylvania.* Oxford, PA: Friends of Oxford Public Library, 1999.

Bradley, John. *The Dickey Family and the Growth of Oxford and Hopewell.* Elkton, MD: C & L Printing, 1990.

Cadbury, Henry J. "Negro Membership in the Society of Friends," *Journal of Negro History,* 21 (1936): 151-213.

Drake, Thomas E. *Quakers and Slavery in America.* New Haven: Yale University, 1950.

Ecenbarger, William. *Walkin' the Line: A Journey from Past to Present Along the Mason-Dixon.* New York: M. Evans & Co., Inc., 2000.

Douglass, Frederick. *My Bondage and My Freedom (1855)* reprinted by Dover Publications, New York, 1969.

Downey, Dennis B. & Raymond Miltyser. *No Crooked Death. Coatesville, Pennsylvania and the Lynching of Zachariah Walker.* Chicago: University of Illinois Press, 1996.

Emilio, Luis F. *A Brave Black Regiment. History of the 54th Massachusetts Regiment (1894)* reprinted by Ayer Company, Salem, NH, 1990.

Evans, David. *Journal: 1838-1890.* Chester County Historical Society.

Foner, Philip S. & George S. Walker, eds. *Proceedings of the Black State Conventions, 1840-1865.* Philadelphia: Temple University Press, 1979.

Forbes, Ella. *But We Have No Country: The 1851 Christiana Resistance.* Cherry Hill, NJ: Africana Homestead Legacy Publishers, 1998.

Franklin, John Hope. *The Emancipation Proclamation.* New York: Doubleday, 1963.

Franklin, John Hope. *From Slavery to Freedom: A History of Negro Americans.* 5th ed. New York: Alfred A. Knopf, 1980

Franklin, John Hope & Loren Schweninger. *Runaway Slaves. Rebels on the Plantation.* New York: Oxford University, 1999.

Futhey, J. Smith & Gilbert Cope. *History of Chester County.* Philadelphia: J.B. Lippincott, 1881.

Gara, Larry. *Liberty Line: The Legend of the Underground Railroad.* Lexington, KY: University of Kentucky Press, 1961.

Hardy, Charles. "The Ku Klux Klan in Pennsylvania." Unpublished paper delivered at the Pennsylvania Academy of Fine Arts on July 17, 1997.

Harper, Douglas R. *"If Thee Must Fight" A Civil War History of Chester County, Pennsylvania.* West Chester, PA: Chester County Historical Society, 1990.

Harper, Douglas R. *West Chester To 1865: That Elegant & Notorious Place.* West Chester, PA: Chester County Historical Society, 1999.

Horton, James O. *Free People of Color. Inside the African American Community.* Washington D.C. Smithsonian, 1993.

Horton, James O. & Lois E. Horton. *In Hope of Liberty. Culture, Community and Protest Among Northern Free Blacks, 1700-1860.* New York: Oxford University, 1997.

Horton, James O. & Lois E. Horton. *Hard Road to Freedom.* New Brunswick, NJ: Rutgers University Press, 2001.

Kashatus, William C. *A Virtuous Education. William Penn's Vision for Philadelphia's Schools.* Wallingford, PA: Pendle Hill, 1997.

Lapsansky, Emma. *Black Presence in Pennsylvania. "Making It Home."* University Park, PA: Pennsylvania Historical Association, 1990.

Lewis, Joseph J. *A Memoir of Enoch Lewis.* West Chester, PA: F.S. Hickman, 1882.

Marietta, Jack. *The Reformation of American Quakerism, 1748-1783.* Philadelphia: University of Pennsylvania, 1984.

Mann, Horace Bond. *Education for Freedom: A History of Lincoln University, PA.* Princeton: Princeton University, 1976.

Mayer, Henry. *All On Fire. William Lloyd Garrison and the Abolition of Slavery.* New York: St. Martin's Press, 1998.

McGowan, James A. *Station Master on the Underground Railroad: The Life and Letters of Thomas Garrett.* Moylan, PA: Whimsie Press, 1977.

Miller, Florence S. *A Legacy of Learning. The History of West Chester Area Schools.* West Chester, PA: West Chester Area School District, 1994.

Murray, Pauli. *Proud Shoes.* New York: Harper Brothers, 1956.

Nash, Gary B. *Forging Freedom: The Formation of Philadelphia's Black Community, 1720-1840.* Cambridge, MA: Harvard University, 1988.

Nash, Gary B. & Jean R. Soderlund. *Freedom By Degrees. Emancipation in Pennsylvania and its Aftermath.* New York: Oxford University, 1991.

Parker, William, "Freedman's Story," *Atlantic Monthly* 17 (February 1866): 165-69.

Patten, William C. "The Anti-Slavery Movement in Chester County." MA Thesis, University of Delaware, 1963.

Pennypacker, Samuel W. *Annals of Phoenixville and its Vicinity: From the Settlement to the Year 1871.* Philadelphia: Bavis & Pennypacker, 1872.

Pennsylvania Yearly Meeting of Progressive Friends, *Proceedings, 1853-1865.* Friends Historical Library, Swarthmore College.

Pinsker, Matthew. "Vigilance in Pennsylvania: Underground Railroad Activities in the Keystone State, 1837-1861," Context Study for the Pennsylvania Historical and Museum Commission, 2000.

Rhodes, Jane. *Mary Ann Shadd Cary. The Black Press and Protest in the Nineteenth Century.* Bloomington, IN: Indiana University, 1998.

Ripley, C. Peter, Larry Gara & Brenda Stevenson. *The Underground Railroad.* Washington D.C.: United States Department of the Interior, National Park Service, 1998.

Rodebaugh, Paul A. *Chester County Notebook.* West Chester, PA: Taggart Printing, 1987.

Rodebaugh, Paul A. *West Chester, the First 200 Years: 1799 - 1999.* West Chester, PA: West Chester Bicentennial History Committee, 1999.

Russo, Paul. "Hinsonville, 1829-1868: A Sketch of a Chester County Afro-American Community," Unpublished manuscript, 1974. Lincoln University Archives.

Siebert, Wilbur H. *The Underground Railroad, From Slavery to Freedom.* New York: Arno Press, 1968.

Slaughter, Thomas P. *Bloody Dawn: The Christiana Riot and Racial Violence in the Antebellum North.* New York: Oxford University, 1991.

Smedley, R.C. *History of the Underground Railroad in Chester and Neighboring Counties.* Lancaster, PA, 1883.

Smith, Billy G. & Richard Wojtowicz, *Blacks Who Stole Themselves. Advertisements for Runaways in the Pennsylvania Gazette, 1728-1790.* Philadelphia: University of Pennsylvania, 1989.

Soderlund, Jean R. *Quakers and Slavery. A Divided Spirit.* Princeton: Princeton University, 1985.

Stampp, Kenneth M. *The Peculiar Institution. Slavery in the Ante-Bellum South.* New York: Vintage, 1956.

Still, William. *The Underground Railroad (1872)* reprinted by Johnson Publishing Company, Chicago, 1970.

Switala, William J. *Underground Railroad in Pennsylvania.* Mechanicsburg, PA: Stackpole Books, 2001.

Taylor, Frances Cloud. *The Trackless Trail. The Story of the Underground Railroad in Kennett Square, Chester County, Pennsylvania, and the Surrounding Community.* Kennett Square, PA, 1976.

Taylor, Frances Cloud. *The Trackless Trail Leads On. An Exploration of Conductors and Their Stations.* Kennett Square, PA, 1995.

Taylor, George W. *Autobiography.* Philadelphia, 1871.

Trueblood, D. Elton. *Abraham Lincoln: Theologian of American Anguish.* New York: Harper & Row, 1973.

Turner, Edward R. *The Negro in Pennsylvania. Slavery - Servitude - Freedom, 1639-1861.* New York: Negro Universities Press, 1910.

Wahl, Albert John. "The Congregational or Progressive Friends in the Pre-Civil War Reform Movement." PhD Dissertation, Temple University, 1951.

Washington, Joseph R. *Black Religion: The Negro and Christianity in the United States.* Boston: Beacon Press, 1964.

Wills, Garry. *Lincoln at Gettysburg: The Words That Remade America.* New York: Simon & Schuster, 1992.

Wold, Margaret L. *A History of West Whiteland.* Exton, PA: West Whiteland Historical Commission, 1982.

Woodson, Carter G. *The History of the Negro Church.* Washington D.C.: Associated Publishers, 1921.

Woodward, Wayne C. *Congress: The Chester County Line.* West Chester, PA: Chester County Historical Society, 1992.

Ziglar, William. "Community on Trial: The Coatesville Lynching of 1911," *Pennsylvania Magazine of History and Biography,* (April 1982): 245-70.

Index

Q

R

S

Acknowledgements

Just Over the Line: Chester County and the Underground Railroad was an extraordinary undertaking for the Chester County Historical Society. Without the support, guidance, and financial assistance of many individuals the exhibition would never have come to fruition. CCHS president and director Roland H. Woodward and the Board of Trustees supported the project from its beginnings in the summer of 1999. Their encouragement and support was vital to its success.

A team of seven consultants were indispensable to the interpretive development of the exhibition, including this publication. Christopher Densmore, curator of Friends Historical Library, Swarthmore College; Larry Gara, emeritus professor of history, Wilmington College; Lois Horton, professor of sociology, George Mason University; Emma Lapsansky, curator of the Quaker Collection, Haverford College; James McGowan, the biographer of Thomas Garrett; Kym Rice, assistant director of museum studies, George Washington University; and Carl Westmoreland, director of external affairs, National Underground Railroad Freedom Center all made critical contributions to the catalogue, scripting and design of the exhibition, and to the process of working with the larger public in order to gain their feedback on our plans. Others read and commented on various chapters of the catalogue, including J. William Frost of Friends Historical Library, Swarthmore College; James McPherson of Princeton University; Paul Rodebaugh; and Thomas Slaughter of Notre Dame University. Still others served as valuable community advisors, including: Bettye F. Baker, Exton; Donald O.H. Brown, Philadelphia; Doris A. Bond, West Chester NAACP; Dr. Charles H. Butler, Coatesville NAACP; The Honorable Clifford E. DeBaptiste, West Chester; Mary Dugan, Kennett Underground Railroad Center; Reverend C. Matthew Hudson, Lincoln University; Lou Mandich, Kennett Underground Railroad Center; Peggy Morscheck, Quaker Information Center; Catherine C. Quillman, *The Philadelphia Inquirer;* J. Justin and Gwen Ragsdale, Philadelphia; Cheryl Rice-Moore, Bear, Delaware; Frances Taylor, Kennett Square; James Trotman, Ph.D., West Chester University; Richard J. Webster, Ph.D., West Chester University; Jacqueline Wiggins, Philadelphia; Terri Wilford, Lionville Middle School; and Emery Wimbish, Lincoln University. Their constructive guidance, constant encouragement and support were greatly appreciated. Any errors of fact or omission that may exist cannot be attributed to them, but rather to me.

A special debt of gratitude is owed the entire staff of Chester County Historical Society, in particular curator Ellen Endslow, and Suzanne Halstead, Barbara Jobe, and Sarah Wesley—my colleagues in the public programs department—whose dedication to the exhibition and invariable good humor got me through some trying times. Other important contributions were made by Mike Dolan, Rob Lukens, Kelsey Murdoch, Pam Powell, Diane Rofini, Laurie Rofini, and Jeff Rollison.

The project staff is very appreciative of the fine design work done for the exhibition by Sanderson Caesar, and the Gecko Group, especially Ellie Byrom-Haley, Kathy Hughes, and Karen Watkins. We are also grateful to those institutions and individuals who loaned artifacts to the exhibition.

Thanks are also due to Suzanne DeMott Gaadt of Gaadt Perspectives, LLC, for the design and development of the exhibition catalogue; D. Loyd Pakradooni of Pearl Pressman Liberty Communications Group for the printing of the catalogue; and to Peter Potter, editor at Penn State University Press, who agreed to market and distrubute the catalogue, creating greater exposure for the exhibition than we would have otherwise enjoyed.

Without the generous and sustained financial support of The William Penn Foundation, *Just Over the Line* would not have been possible. We are grateful for the assistance of Olive Mosier, in particular. The project has also received generous support from the Commonwealth of Pennsylvania's Department of Community and Economic Development, via the initiative of Senator James W. Gerlach, Senator Robert J. Thompson, Representative Elinor Z. Taylor, and Representative Chris Ross; the Clamer Foundation; Chester County Conference & Visitors Bureau; and the Chace Fund of the Philadelphia Yearly Meeting of the Religious Society of Friends.

Finally, a special thanks to Sarah and Charles Northrop whose Quaker hospitality and friendship were greatly appreciated during my several trips out to the National Underground Railroad Freedom Center in Cincinnati; and to my family—Jackie, Tim, Peter, and Ben—whose steadfast support and unconditional love saw me through the difficult times.

About *the* Author

William C. Kashatus is director of public programs at Chester County Historical Society. A graduate of Earlham College, he earned his M.A. at Brown University and his Ph.D. at the University of Pennsylvania.

Before coming to CCHS, Kashatus taught history for fifteen years in Philadelphia's independent schools, including Abington Friends School, The Episcopal Academy, and the William Penn Charter School. During that time, he spent his summers as an historical interpreter at Valley Forge and Independence National Historical Parks.

Kashatus' books include: *A Virtuous Education: William Penn's Vision of Philadelphia's Schools* and *Connie Mack's '29 Triumph: The Rise and Fall of the Philadelphia Athletics Dynasty.* He has also published more than 200 essays in such periodicals as *American History Magazine, Pennsylvania Heritage, Pennsylvania Magazine of History and Biography, The Philadelphia Daily News, The Philadelphia Inquirer,* and *Quaker History.*